RED
DWARF
W9-BSR-624

THE OFFICIAL RED DWARF COMPANION
ISBN 1 85286 456 7

Published by
Titan Books Ltd
19 Valentine Place
London SE1 8QH

First edition October 1992
10 9 8 7 6 5 4 3 2



A CIP record for this publication is available from the British Library.

ACKNOWLEDGEMENTS
Many thanks to everyone who helped out with this book. In particular, Rob Grant and Doug Naylor, Paul Jackson, Ed Bye, Craig Charles, Chris Barrie, Robert Llewellyn, Danny John-Jules, Hattie Hayridge, Peter Wragg, Mel Bibby, Andria Pennell, Howard Burden, Mike Butcher at *Red Dwarf Magazine* and Nic Farey at the Red Dwarf Fan Club. Special thanks to Kate Cotton at Noel Gay and Roger Sabin in Clapham for services above and beyond the call of duty.

*Bruce Dessau, London, 1992.*

**PICTURE CREDITS:**

Warwick Bedford 35-37, 39-41; Howard Burden 88, 89; Paul Grant 6, 15, 19, 23, 27, 30, 31-32, 43-49, 66, 67, 70, 71, 73, 74, 75, 76, 79, 87, 90, 91; Chris Ridley 4, 8, 12; Mike Vaughan 7, 9-11, 13-14, 16-18, 20-22, 24-26, 28-29, 30, 33, 51-65, 66, 68, 69, 71, 72, 74, 75, 76, 77-78, 79, 86, 88, 89, 91, 96; Peter Wragg collection 68, 69, 70, 73, 80-85, 91

**Pages 92-93:** videos courtesy of BBC Video, T-shirt courtesy of BMS Merchandising, comic courtesy of Fleetway Editions Ltd and books courtesy of Penguin Books.

**Front cover:** Chris Ridley.

**Back cover:** Mike Vaughan, except for 'The Last Day' photo by Paul Grant.



Printed and bound by Stephens & George Limited, Merthyr Tydfil, Mid Glamorgan.

by

**BRUCE DESSAU**

introduction by

**ROB GRANT** and **DOUG NAYLOR**

**TITAN BOOKS**

# CONTENTS

# GENESIS

*"Why did no-one mention this before? If I'd been told about this at the start..."*

**- Rimmer**

**THE EIGHT** year-old boy with the leaky-pen mouth knocked timidly and entered the Sixth Form common room. In his hand he clutched a twelve page punishment essay entitled 'Knocking Over Sixth Formers' Coffee Mugs'. After ignoring him for a suitably humiliating amount of time, the prefect in the brown Hush Puppies and the black barathea blazer turned and took the essay.

"So you've done it, have you?" he said. "How long did it take?"

"I was up till nearly midnight," the boy whimpered.

Without even glancing at the pages, the prefect tore the essay into eight and dropped it into the bin. The rest of the Sixth Form howled with derision and pelted the prefect with rugby boots, books and rubbers.

The prefect's name was Rimmer.

Two Sixth Formers sat in the corner, playing their fifth game of chess of the day. They had perhaps twenty minutes before lunch break ended and double history began. Twenty minutes before they would be forced to skive off to their favourite coffee bar and spend the afternoon smoking No 6 and finalising their thoughts on the meaning of life. The one with the distinctly non-regulation flared trousers and Peter Wyngarde sideburns was called Grant. The one with the plastic Chelsea boots and the *Man from UNCLE* polo neck was called Naylor. They didn't know it, but something significant had just taken place. Neither of them would mention the incident again for twelve years.

Fade out.

*" ... lying on your bunk, reading 'What Bike?' and eating Sugar Puff sandwiches for eight hours every day ... "* - Rimmer

*"This sounds like a twelve change-of-underwear trip!"*
- Cat

Fade in.

It's two o'clock in the morning. In eight hours' time, we are going to start rehearsals for a radio sketch show called *Son of Cliché*. Half the show remains unwritten. In less than sixteen hours, 400 people are going to show up at the Paris Theatre in London to watch the recording of a show that, as yet, only half exists.

There is a feeling beyond panic, beyond fear, where your emotions run full circle and you actually start to feel euphoric.

This is happening to us.

We begin to giggle hysterically. Almost certainly our career is over and it's all our fault. Three cast members, a musical director, a producer and his PA and eight technicians are sleeping soundly in the knowledge that the script will be delivered, since we've been assuring them all for a week that it's simply a question of dotting a few 'i's and crossing the odd 't'.

We've been lying.

We've just spent the last three months working seven days a week on a TV series for Jasper Carrott, and then had to segue straight into a two-show-a-week commitment for a radio sketch series written entirely by us. It's an absurd schedule and more assertive people than us would probably have been able to get out of it. But, not wanting to disappoint anyone, somehow we've agreed to do it.

And the last amusing sketch in the universe has been written. There are no more funny ideas to be had.

Then, suddenly, out of this emotional cocktail of panic, hysteria, exhaustion and terror, we write a sketch called 'Dave Hollins - Space Cadet'. It concerns the plight of a lone space traveller and his computer, the rest of the crew having been wiped out by a strange, chameleonic alien.

At last, we're up and running. We finish the rest of the show and turn up with the script, having creased and folded it to make it look like it's at least a week old, apart from the occasional dotted 'i' and crossed 't'. And the only half clue that we've been up all night is that, on separate occasions, we both walk off the edge of the stage and crash into the orchestra pit.

The audience arrive. The show begins. And, as is sometimes the way with these things, the show is actually better than some of those we've spent weeks and weeks writing and rewriting. They laugh at everything. But far and away the hit of the show is a sketch called 'Dave Hollins - Space Cadet'.

Fade out.

*"Remember, it's Rimmer's mind out there*

*... expect sickness."*

**- Lister**

*"I want you to be unpleasant, cruel and sarcastic ..."*

**- Lister**

Fade in.

We sit across the table from Jimmy Gilbert, the Head of Light Entertainment, BBC TV. We tell him we've got an idea for a situation comedy. It's about four students sharing a house together. He's a nice man and sounds genuinely interested. He says, however, the BBC have just made a situation comedy which sounds a bit like that, called *The Young Ones*. We say we're sure it'll be nothing like ours. We want ours to star this weird stand-up comic we've seen called Nigel Planer.

Any other ideas, he prompts.

Well, there's this project we've been working on which we think could be very, very funny indeed. It's called *POW* and it's set in a Japanese prisoner of war camp. It'll be absolutely real, with integrity; no funny torturers. Sort of *King Rat*, with laughs.

He gently suggests we write something from our own experience. Something we know about.

We leave and spend the next two years writing for TV sketch shows and thinking about it.

We return with a situation comedy, set on a space ship based on a certain sketch from *Son of Cliché*, about two ordinary guys trapped together in a boring job, of which we have vast experience. Jimmy Gilbert reads the script and likes it very much indeed. Unfortunately, by this time he has left the BBC, and his replacement hates it very much indeed.

Fade out.

"Oh, that is just so superb, sir. How do you do it?

... It's total genius."

- Kryten

Fade in.

Three years later, Paul Jackson called us on his new mobile phone from a Manchester-London train:

"Hi guys, it's ... *kkktktktttttttttk static, crackle kkkkkktttttttkk* ..."

"Hello?"

"I'm calling from a *kkktktk-ttttttttttk more static, crackle kkkkttttttkk* ... train."

"Paul? Is that you?"

"I'll phone you *kkktktktttttttttk* ... back ... *kkkkkktttttttkk* ... OK?"

The phone rang again.

"Is that better?"

"Much better."

"I've just been to BBC Manchester and they've read the script."

"Yes?"

"And they haven't said no."

"They haven't said no?"

"Yes."

"Is that good?"

"Oh yes. That's how these things work."

"They haven't said yes, then?"

"No, but they haven't said no, and if they continue not to say no, we're in."

And he was right. We were in. Three years after *Red Dwarf* was rejected by the BBC, the same script was accepted and commissioned by BBC Manchester.

**OF ALL** the shows we've worked on in television, *Red Dwarf* is the most complex, logistically and technically, to realise. In comparison, normal sitcoms are a total doddle. It's easy enough to write three Listers and three Rimmers appearing together in the same scene from different timezones, or scenes where Kryten's disembodied hand goes for a stroll, or Starbug crashes into an arctic moon: it's another matter altogether making it possible. With a tight budget and an even tighter schedule, there is only one way to make it work, and that's to have the best production team around. Fortunately, we've got it. From the very bottom of our rehydration units, we thank them all.

The one key person who isn't interviewed in this book is Ed Bye, who directed the first four series. Without him, it would never have worked or been half the success it has. Which isn't to say we're not glad to see the back of him - good riddance to the old bastard. He was too tall anyway.

***Rob Grant and Doug Naylor,***
*Nodnol 2991.*

**"You've heard of this ... ?"**

**- Rimmer**

*"Only as a myth, a dark fable, a horror tale told ... wherever hardened space dogs gather to drink fermented vegetable products ..."* - Kryten

# LISTER

**RED DWARF PERSONNEL FILES SUBJECT NO 1:**

**NAME:** David Lister

**TYPE:** Human

**RANK:** Third technician

**LIKES:** Kippers and vindaloos

**DISLIKES:** Arnold Judas Rimmer

**FIRST LOVE:** Christine Kochanski

**SKILLS:** Able to belch 'Yankee Doodle Dandy'

**DAVE LISTER** wasn't exactly cut out for space travel. The street smart gimboid's academic career reached the giddy heights of ninety -seven minutes at art college. Lister left when he found out there were lectures - first thing in the after-noon - and after 3,000,000 years in stasis, work is still a four-letter word.

For Lister, life on the Red Dwarf Mining Ship is spent salvaging space wrecks, playing poker and eating curry - without much sal-vaging. Lister hates Rimmer, but it's driving the supercilious holo-gram nuts that keeps him sane.

Over the years, Lister has emerged as the good guy of Red Dwarf. Then again, he is the only human being still alive. Perhaps that's why he has ceased to worry about his appearance. As the ship has travelled deeper into space, Lister's original issue fatigues have been superseded by the scuzziest sartorial off-cuts in the universe. On important occasions Lister wears his special T-shirt - the one with only two curry stains - and boxer-shorts that actually bend.

Despite a tendency towards melancholia, Lister has become resigned to his galactic fate. He no longer dreams of setting up a farm in Fiji and he finally seems to have got over his cosmic crush on Chrissie Kochanski. If it wasn't for Arnold Rimmer always getting in the way, Lister could almost be content bumming around the uni-verse for all eternity.

"He's become the social worker of the crew. Believe it or not, he's the most well-balanced of a bad bunch"

Rob Grant illustrates the thin dividing line between actor and character. "We were having breakfast in the BBC canteen. Craig joined us and said he was worried about people thinking he really was Lister. While he was talking, he took a sausage off Danny's plate, squirted some tomato ketchup straight onto the Formica table, dipped the sausage in the ketchup, and ate it. 'I mean,' he chewed, 'I'm nothing like him, really.' Danny laughed so hard, he almost choked to death."

The amazing thing is that Dave Lister, er Craig Charles, didn't realise what he was doing. If there's one risk about starring in a long-running successful series, it's that your alter ego can sometimes start taking you over.

Of course, as Craig Charles recalls, he might not have got the part of Lister at all: "I'd done *Saturday Night Live* with Paul Jackson, and one day Paul lent me a *Red Dwarf* script. He wasn't offering me a part, he just wanted me to tell him if I thought the Cat was racist. I said I didn't think so, and I wouldn't mind auditioning for Lister. At the time, all these diva actors were up for Lister. Alfred Molina had apparently been given it, but they seemed to think I kicked off Chris (Barrie), so they offered me the part."

Despite a shared penchant for sausages à la table, Craig Charles doesn't believe there is too much overlap between him and Lister: "The accent's the same but it's not actually written as Liverpudlian, Rob and Doug made a point of not having any Liverpool slang in it. Instead, they came up with things like 'smeghead'."

As *Red Dwarf* has developed, Lister's character has matured. He is still partial to vindaloos, kippers and Christine Kochanski, but his outfit has changed from cheap cotton slacks to chunky Mad Max leathers and his psychological make-up has become more complex. "He's changed in every series," explains Charles. "Now he's older and wiser, he's become the social worker of the crew. Believe it or not, he's the most well-balanced of a bad bunch. Rimmer is just a wrecked mass of neuroses."

While most of the action in recent episodes has happened to Rimmer, Charles believes that Lister has become the anchor role: "Even if it's a Rimmer story, it's seen through Lister's eyes, and it's all about Lister's reactions and his moral codes." When it comes to his favourite episode, he feels: "Everyone talks about 'Backwards', but 'Marooned' was my favourite. I'm very fond of 'Timeslides' too".

Grant and Naylor have the main input into Lister's psyche, but Charles contributes too: "I suppose the guys write Lister from personal traits of my own. They watch the way we individually react to things and take them on board, so our characters are very close - we feel like we actually are them really. I suppose I am a bit like Lister - in the nicest possible way, of course." ■

# RIMMER

**RED DWARF PERSONNEL FILES SUBJECT NO 2:**

**NAME:** Arnold J. Rimmer

**TYPE:** Hologram

**RANK:** Second technician

**LIKES:** Reggie Wilson and his Hammond Organ

**DISLIKES:** Gazpacho soup

**FIRST LOVE:** Yvonne McGruder

**SKILLS:** Being dead as a can of Spam

**ARNOLD JUDAS** Rimmer started life as a tragic smeghead and ended up dead: as a tragic smeghead hologram. He left home at sixteen to become an officer and a gentleman and ended up as a chicken soup machine operative. Even in this lowly position he was responsible for inadvertently killing the entire crew of Red Dwarf: his punishment is to spend eternity as a hologram denied the power of touch.

The problem for the surviving members is Rimmer's personality has stayed exactly the same - he was, and is, a petty-minded, jumped-up, anal-retentive megalomaniac with delusions of competence. While the others enjoy all-night card sessions, he takes his pleasure in solo games of Risk, playing with his collection of model soldiers and jogging around the ship. Not the universe's most fun individual.

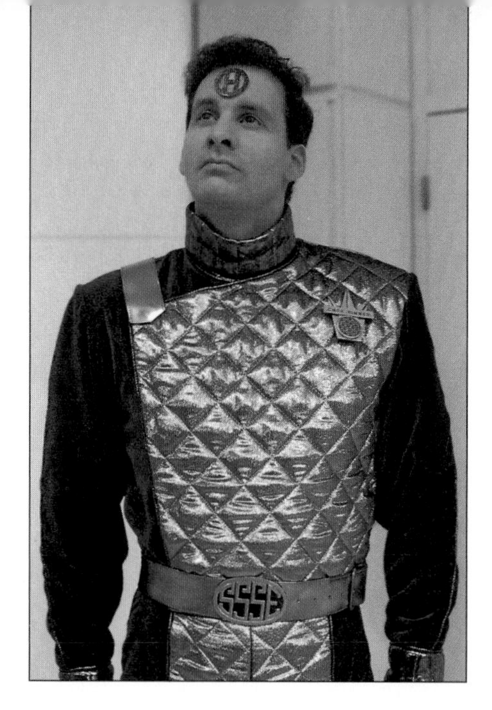

But there's a pathetic side to his character. He knows he's at the bottom of the metaphorical slime-bucket, and even when he has the opportunity to remedy his sexual inexperience and have sex twice a day with a beautiful female hologram, events conspire against him.

After five series of *Red Dwarf*, Rimmer continues to excel as the ship's token tosspot. We've learnt all there is to know about him and he is less lovable than ever.

Despite his lack of acting experience, Barrie was clearly ready to play a man as dead as a can of Spam. He'd got his Equity card doing impressions on the stand-up circuit, having been sacked from every previous job he'd ever had, and since then the work has just snowballed. These days he juggles *Red Dwarf* with both the recording of BBC1's *The Brittas Empire* and providing a multitude of voices for commercials.

Over the years, Barrie has intimately observed the evolution of Rimmer. It hasn't been a pretty sight: "In the early days he was looked upon as a sheer bastard for no apparent reason. But he's dead and can't touch things, which is a good enough reason for being bad-tempered, fed-up and grumpy. But we couldn't always have him saying: 'By the way, I'm dead, which is why I'm being such a git', so the other thing was to have horrible things, like the sacrificial virgin thing in 'Terrorform', happen to him."

**"In the early days he was looked upon as a sheer bastard..."**

Having friends in high places is not always a guarantee of career advancement. Chris Barrie was well-known to Rob Grant and Doug Naylor through his work with them on radio and then *Carrott's Lib*. By the time *Red Dwarf* was in the pipeline, Barrie was working with Grant and Naylor on *Spitting Image*. Yet, when the writers were casting the series the voice-over king was barely in the running.

Barrie takes up the story: "I think Rob, Doug and Paul Jackson were in two minds whether to do it with legitimate actors or people they'd worked with in the past, and I fell into the latter camp. Eventually I got a letter saying, 'Thanks, but we're going with legitimate actors'. Then three weeks later they decided to go with us lot."

Chris Barrie believes that sometimes you can forget what a gimboid Rimmer really is: "You only realise what a complete dingbat Arnie is when you meet Ace Rimmer and see what he would have been like if he had been successful. What we are ultimately trying to say is that Rimmer is pathetic really, and it is probably better to feel sorry for him than to hate him. Rimmer gives you a reason to hate the others, because they are so horrible to him. But, at the end, if he wins something, there's always a glint in his eye that says: 'I'm a bastard after all, and I hate these three smegheads.'"

Barrie also has to cope with the familiar TV ailment, where fans write to the actor confusing him with the character: "Strangely, I don't get many proposals of marriage, but a lot of people want to know about me. Some want me to draw around my palm and send it back. Some want to know how old I was when I ate my first Topic bar. And some want to know how I felt when I went into stasis for the third time. I think they feel sorry for me."

Fortunately for him, the similarities between Barrie and Rimmer, despite a remarkable physical resemblance, are minimal: "Rimmer is a dreamer, but he is brought down to earth in every episode and realises that he is a complete smeghead. It always ends with his ego shrinking down to the size of a small radish."

Barrie is hard-pressed to come up with one favourite episode. In *Red Dwarf V* things hotted up for him in 'Holoship' when Rimmer actually had sex and fell in love, but every series had equally high points: "I loved 'Better Than Life' and 'Dimension Jump', doing Ace Rimmer was a good acting challenge, being a James Bond character with a silly wig."

Despite the continued success of *The Brittas Empire*, Barrie has no intention of hanging up his spacesuit: "*Dwarf* is a real one-off, in that I'm part of a team. I don't want to give it up. I don't mind playing these losers because they are classic British fall guys. And you know something, eventually you do start liking Rimmer because he is so sad. The saddest character ever." ■

***"Eventually you do start liking Rimmer because he is so sad. The saddest character ever"***

# KRYTEN

**RED DWARF PERSONNEL FILES SUBJECT NO 3:**

**NAME:** Kryten

**TYPE:** Service Mechanoid

**RANK:** Ditto

**LIKES:** Serving Red Dwarf crew

**DISLIKES:** Not programmed to 'dislike'

**FIRST LOVE:** Camille

**SKILLS:** Alternates as superb vacuum cleaner

**KRYTEN STARTS** life in *Red Dwarf* as a Series 400 mechanoid with a problem. He'd been programmed to serve but he doesn't have anyone to serve - his previous crew on the Nova 5 were skeletons with about as much meat on them as a Chicken McNugget. The Red Dwarf survivors redeploy him on their ship - Rimmer, in particular, taking advantage of Kryten's handy 'I serve therefore I am' philosophy, gives him a planet-sized list of domestic chores.

Fortunately for Kryten, Lister takes him under his wing and teaches him how to rebel. No longer a silicon doormat, the rubberised robot ditches his frilly apron, paints a portrait of Rimmer on the toilet, mounts Lister's bike and turns into Marlon Brando in *The Wild One.*

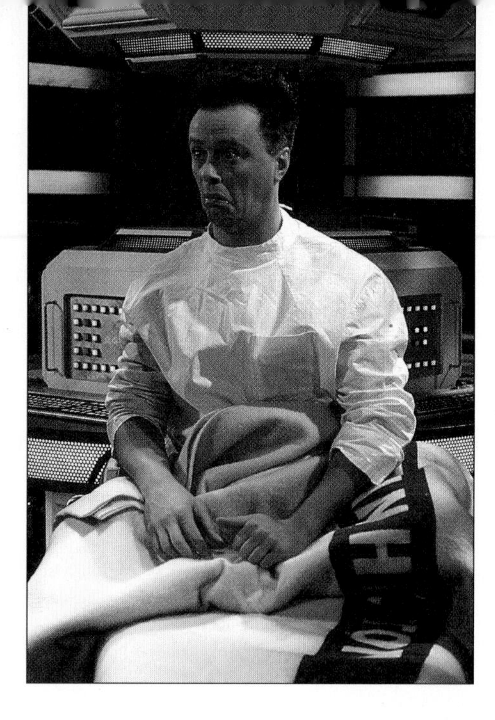

Kryten returns in *Red Dwarf III* with a mid-Atlantic accent and a body made of reinforced plastic, becoming an integral part of the crew. Rimmer even attempts to teach him to fly Starbug 1, but nerves play merry hell with Kryten's anxiety chip, and he ends up taking the ship through a Time Hole and onto another version of Earth. Since these shaky beginnings, however, Kryten has gone on to become the team's most resourceful member.

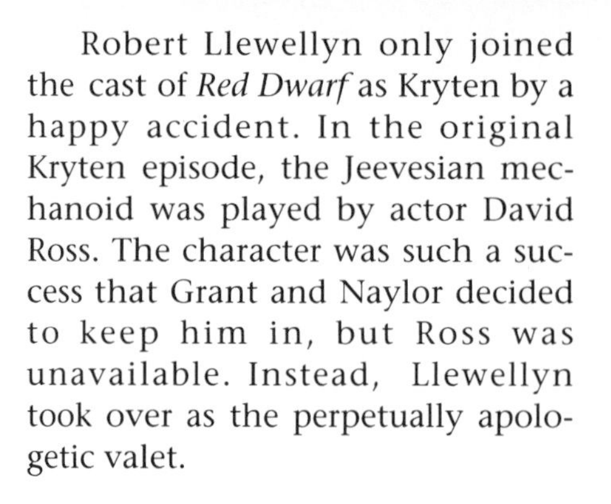

Robert Llewellyn only joined the cast of *Red Dwarf* as Kryten by a happy accident. In the original Kryten episode, the Jeevesian mechanoid was played by actor David Ross. The character was such a success that Grant and Naylor decided to keep him in, but Ross was unavailable. Instead, Llewellyn took over as the perpetually apologetic valet.

Grant and Naylor are primarily responsible for Kryten's eccentric behaviour, but Llewellyn - who is a writer himself - makes contributions too: "It's pretty much their baby, but it is also a joint effort. Rob and Doug are good to work with because they will accept suggestions. If I do a funny walk or a silly voice - like in 'DNA', when one of my spare heads had a northern accent - they write that into the script."

As the plots have thickened and the characters expanded, Llewellyn has had to learn more lines: "I think Rob and Doug enjoy seeing me walking for hours up and down the corridor. And Kryten's lines are often incredibly complex, with no logical flow, which makes it even harder. It's definitely the hardest thing I've ever done in my life. I think it's a subtle form of torture."

**"It's definitely the hardest thing I've ever done in my life. I think it's a subtle form of torture"**

Unlike the others, Kryten has to go through the weekly ordeal of being fully made up until Llewellyn is completely unrecognisable: "That's the toughest part of the gig without a doubt. They've got it down to two hours now. The first time it took about six, then it was four. Which means if you are starting at 9am - which I never did, because it meant being in the make-up chair by 5am - it is very debilitating and tiring. I complain an enormous amount - it's the way I get through the day, by moaning and whingeing."

Despite joining the programme late, Kryten has inspired devoted clones of his own. Some people attend recordings of the programme at Shepperton Studios with an 'H' stuck to their forehead, but that's nothing compared to the lengths fans go to to emulate the intergalactic serf. "One woman had a cardboard Kryten mask that was really well-made," recalls Llewellyn. "The top of her head was completely square."

Llewellyn's favourite episode is 'Polymorph', where he had the hoover attachment emerging from an unmentionable orifice: "I've never done any performing on a show where I couldn't hear the other performers' lines because people were laughing so much. Craig was shouting and I was right next to him, but I couldn't hear a thing. When Chris/Rimmer had said the line 'You'll bonk anything, Lister' in rehearsals, I can remember being in real physical pain laughing."

Other moments have not been quite as successful: "Did you know Craig's got a solid head? I discovered that in 'Demons and Angels', when there's a bad version of all of us, and there's one scene where the bad Kryten is chasing Lister and I punched two holes in the wall and tried to strangle him. The first time we filmed it, they marked where my fists were going to come through and where he was going to stand because I couldn't see him. I punched quite hard and it felt like I'd hit a brick wall, but it was actually Craig's head. He went flying and I really hurt my hand - and I was wearing a leather glove with studs on it. His head is obviously very solid. But apart from that there haven't been too many mishaps. When I've been blown up, I've had the odd spark get a bit close to me, though - close to the family jewels you know..." ■

# THE CAT

**RED DWARF PERSONNEL FILES SUBJECT NO 4:**

**NAME:** The Cat

**TYPE:** Super-evolved feline

**RANK:** None

**LIKES:** Milk

**DISLIKES:** Creases

**FIRST LOVE:** Himself

**SKILLS:** Able to lick bottom with tongue

**THE CAT** is Red Dwarf's resident fashion victim. After Lister's moggy, Frankenstein, had bred for 3,000,000 years, the result is this preening, purring, felis sapiens - a human being with an abundance of tabby-traits. The Cat loves fishies, hates water, loves milk, hates dogs and, like all creatures of a feline persuasion, has an irrational fear of tank tops. His role on Red Dwarf, apart from being the numero uno fashion expert in the universe, is to look cool and... look cool. Occasionally he has been known to get excited though - it's easy for him to spot the difference, all six of his nipples start tingling.

Poor old Cat, for all his romantic leanings, he is perpetually starved of female company. When the others meet their opposite numbers in 'Parallel Universe', the Cat's opposite turns out to be a flea-ridden descendant of a dog; when the others meet their dream partners in 'Camille', the Cat meets... himself.

It's a tough life for the Cat on Red Dwarf, particularly as the only milk left on board is dog's milk, which lasts a long time because it tastes the same when it goes off and because no bugger will drink it. The Cat may not be the brightest member of the crew, but he does have the most nipples.

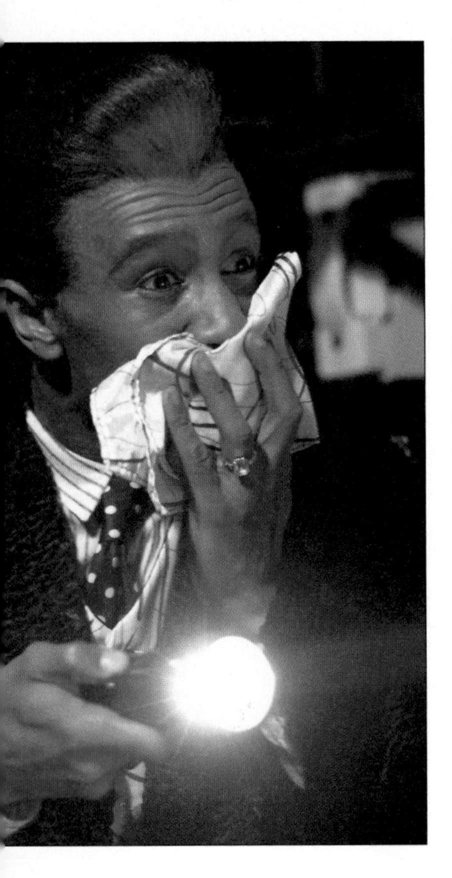

**"His vanity is from Little Richard and the wacky screaming was taken from James Brown"**

Danny John-Jules, who has played the Cat since it was barely out of kitty litter, was the very first person auditioned for *Red Dwarf*. According to John-Jules, Grant and Naylor took one look at him "and they thought, 'THAT is the man'."

Contrary to appearances, the Cat and Danny John-Jules aren't dead ringers. The Cat's high heels give him the impression of height, while John-Jules is rather more modestly proportioned. "I don't get recognised that often," he explains. "People seem to think that the Cat is six foot plus and thin and gangly, but I'm short."

If they ever make the much-mooted American version of *Red Dwarf*, they will have to give the part of the Cat to Prince. The vanity, self-obsession and supreme confidence suggest that the Minneapolis major-domo was a leading inspiration for John-Jules. Apparently not, but the Cat's inspiration does come from a pantheon of performers who also happen to have heavily influenced Prince.

Grant and Naylor came up with the original concept of the Cat, but John-Jules helped with the right moves. "I've based him on a lot of different people. He's a cross between a guy I used to understudy and the American comedian Richard Pryor. His facial expressions are from Richard Pryor and the way he says 'buddy' - Richard Pryor also used to say 'buddy'. His vanity is from Little Richard and the wacky screaming was taken from James Brown. I based the movements - the spins, etc - on a guy that used to send up James Brown."

Unlike the rest of the cast and many of the guest cameos, John-Jules' background is mainly in mainstream showbusiness. As a variety show dancer he backed Dickie Henderson and the very unalternative Jimmy Tarbuck. From there he moved into musicals. Any we might have heard of? *"Cats"*. Also on his

cv are *Starlight Express*, *Time*, *Barnum* and more pantomimes than you can shake a stick at.

As an extrovert and a natural showman, playing the Cat came easily to John-Jules. The only real challenge was the teeth, those tiny fangs that complete the feline fop's appearance: "Originally I just took them home and wore them round the house. The only time I had real difficulties was when I was wearing those teeth as Duane Dibbly in 'Back to Reality'. That was a real mouthful, doing all the dialogue and trying to sound like 'Oh God, he's got a pair of false teeth and that's why he can't speak properly.'"

John-Jules realised fame had finally struck when people started to come up to him in public and ask him to say "Duane Dibbly": "The Duane Dibbly episode was probably my favourite one, because it was a chance to be more versatile and it was a good one because everyone thought *Red Dwarf* was ending." Luckily for the rest of us, it hasn't. Now there's paws for thought. ■

# HOLLY

**RED DWARF PERSONNEL FILES SUBJECT NO 5:**

**NAME:** Holly

**TYPE:** Tenth generation A1 hologrammatic computer

**RANK:** Ditto

**LIKES:** Clean VDU

**DISLIKES:** Static electricity

**FIRST LOVE:** Sinclair ZX81

**SKILLS:** Collector of singing potatoes

RED DWARF

**HOLLY, RED** Dwarf's sardonic computer, is unaffected by the holocaust that decimates the ship's crew. By the time Lister comes out of stasis, the loneliness has got to Holly, who becomes the chief source of information for the survivors between bouts of deadpan gibberish. He is not the brightest computer ever invented, despite a reputed IQ of 6,000.

But he does have a sense of humour: as a 'wheeze of the week', he pretends to get all his knowledge from the *Junior Encyclopaedia of Space,* and inflicts upon the crew a 'successor' - the sadistic Queeg. These character traits are continued into series III, when Holly performs a head sex change operation on himself, basing his new face on Hilly, a female computer he had once fallen madly in love with. His screen presence is transformed from a balding middle-aged man to a strawberry blonde female with a Cheshire cat smile - not that this improves his/her intellectual performance, which becomes increasingly erratic with the passing of time.

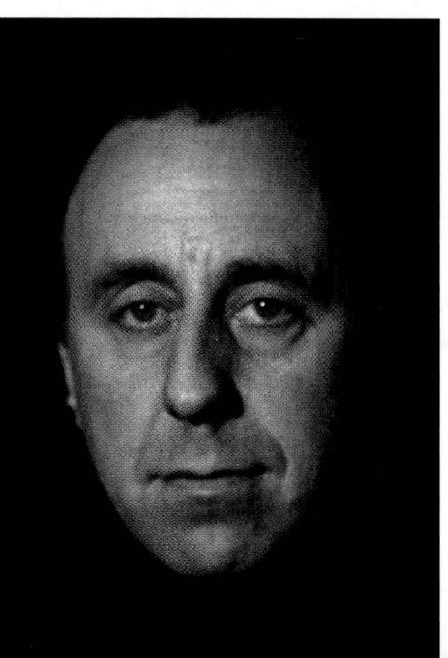

The ship's computer started life as a man, played by Norman Lovett, and has ended up as a woman, played by Hattie Hayridge. What was even more confusing, but inscrutably clever, was that Hattie Hayridge had already been introduced as Holly's female alter ego, Hilly, in 'Parallel Universe'. Confused? You will be. It was Paul Jackson who first thought of Hattie Hayridge as the female Norman Lovett. She had the same lugubrious quality and the kind of unemotional voice that was a prerequisite for the jumped-up Filofax. In the end, about ten other performers were auditioned, but Hayridge landed the role.

Holly's significance in the series has, however, dwindled as the programme has grown. When the action was set predominantly in the drive room, Holly was on hand with dithering advice, but a lack of mobility has seen a lot of the expositionary lines previously delivered by Holly handed over to Kryten. Hattie Hayridge's favourite episode is in fact one which she wasn't in: "It was 'Meltdown', where we landed on the planet with different waxworks. When they were on location, running across landmines, I was in hysterics." ■

# SPECIAL GUESTS

**RED DWARF** has given a leg-up to various other struggling thespians. If you go right back to episode one, 'The End', Christine Kochanski made her first appearance as Lister's obscure object of desire. Pop fans might not have recognised the actress's name, CP Grogan, but they would have recognised the face as lead singer of Scottish pop group Altered Images. Clare Grogan - she changed her name because someone else in Equity had the same name - will also be familiar to film fans as the spiky teenager in *Gregory's Girl*.

*Red Dwarf* seems to be good news for Scottish performers. Celtic comedian Craig Ferguson, more recently sighted presenting the pop show *Friday Night at the Dome*, cropped up as Confidence in, yes, 'Confidence and Paranoia' in March 1988.

*Red Dwarf II* started out by giving another young comedian one of his first breaks in 'Kryten'. Not that you'd ever have spotted Tony Slattery as an android actor in Kryten's favourite soap, 'Androids'. More instantly recognisable was Morwenna Banks, part of Channel 4's *Absolutely* team, who played the lift attendant in 'Stasis Leak'. Another *Absolutely* joker, John Docherty, donned a heavy skull-like disguise to play the Inquisitor in the eponymous episode in *Red Dwarf V*.

The third series of *Red Dwarf* kicked off with 'Backwards', which marked the official debuts of both Hattie Hayridge as Holly and Robert Llewellyn as Kryten. Less easy-to-spot was the cameo by comedian Arthur Smith, one of the customers in the Backwards bar. Frances Barber was recognisable in one of her incarnations as the alien creature in 'Polymorph'. It almost had royalty in it in 'Timeslides', if only Koo Stark had married her one-time boyfriend Prince Andrew and had still been prepared to have constant sex with Lister as Lady Sabrina Mulholland-Jjones. Never mind, there would still have been a cameo by American motormouth Ruby Wax, who played strident news reporter Blaize Falconburger. Wax, of course, was director Ed Bye's wife. Oh, and still keeping it in the family, Craig's younger brother, Emile Charles, played Young Lister.

Series IV's opener, 'Camille', started off with a spot of art imitating life. Lister's love interest was played by Suzanne Rhatigan, while Kryten's love interest was played by Judy Pascoe. In reality, the respective performers are Craig Charles' and Robert Llewellyn's real-life partners. Less romantic was the appearance of Nicholas Ball as the evil gun-toting Simulant in 'Justice'. Real TV buffs may remember Ball as the cockney detective Hazel, though more recently he has returned to the screens as Colin Watkins' long-suffering, short-tempered film producer, Hunter, in *Colin's Sandwich. Red Dwarf IV* culminated in 'Meltdown', in which a whole slew of celebrities, from Marilyn Monroe to Elvis Presley, were played by modern day lookalikes. The most notable of the impersonators was Forbes Masson, who played Stan Laurel and was the star of Channel 4's comedy series *My Dead Dad*.

By the time Grant and Naylor made *Red Dwarf V*, they must have seen Mike Leigh's movie *Life is Sweet*. In episode one the star of Leigh's film, Jane Horrocks, appeared as Lister's hologramatic paramour, Nirvanah Crane; in 'Back to Reality', Timothy Spall, the star of *Auf Wiedersehen Pet* and the ridiculous restaurateur in *Life is Sweet,* put in a late appearance. 'Back to Reality' also saw Lenny Von Dohlen, familiar to *Twin Peaks* fans as Harold Smith, the owner of Laura Palmer's secret diary, make an appearance as The Cop.

Back in 'Holoship', seventies TV fans might have recognised one of the Enlightenment crew, Don Warrington, as the foil of the very unenlightened racist Rigsby in *Rising Damp*. Finally, in 'Terrorform', fashion followers would have spotted Sara Stockbridge, one of the hand-maidens who rubbed oil into Rimmer's pasty body. Stockbridge is best known as designer Vivienne Westwood's favourite model, but is currently pursuing an acting career.

Oh. And really finally, in 'Quarantine' Mr Flibble appeared as himself. ■

**Above far left:** *Frances Barber in 'Polymorph'.*
**Far left:** *Koo Stark as Lady Sabrina Mulholland-Jjones in 'Timeslides'.*
**Above:** *Timothy Spall in 'Back to Reality'.*
**Left:** *Lenny Von Dohlen as The Cop in 'Back to Reality'.*

RIMMER
SECOND
TECHNICIAN

# SEASON ONE

# THE END

**ON THE** mining vessel Red Dwarf, a huge radiation leak kills almost the entire crew. The only survivors are the disorderly Dave Lister, who was in suspended animation during the disaster (sentenced to eighteen months as a "non-event mass with a quantum probability of zero"), and his pregnant cat, who was safely sealed in the ship's hold. Revived 3,000,000 years later, Lister is dismayed to find that his only companions are a narcissistic lifeform who evolved from his cat; Arnold Rimmer, a hologram simulation of his least favourite crew members; and Holly, the ship's dim-witted but indestructible computer. ■

# FUTURE ECHOES

*"Goits, Goits, I'm surrounded by goits."*

**- Rimmer**

**BOREDOM** is taking hold: Rimmer gets various new haircuts and the Cat fishes for robot fish - but breaks a tooth. In desperation, Lister tries to get back to Earth in stasis with the Cat, much to Rimmer's irritation. But the ship breaks the light barrier and encounters time-warps, leading the crew to see their own futures. Lister observes himself as a 171 year-old man and meets his two future twin sons, Jim and Bexley. But how is Lister going to have children when there are no women left in the universe? ■

# BALANCE OF POWER

**THE OFFICIOUS** Rimmer wants everything on ship to be spick and span, but Lister just wants to laze around - preferably with a hologram of his old flame, the lovely Christine Kochanski. Amid much arguing, Lister plans to take the chef's exam in order to pull rank on Rimmer and thus command him to replace the hologram disc with that of Kochanski. Finally, Rimmer gives way. So, now there's no reason why Lister should continue with the exam. Well, yes, actually, there is: Kochanski's body still contains Rimmer's personality. ■

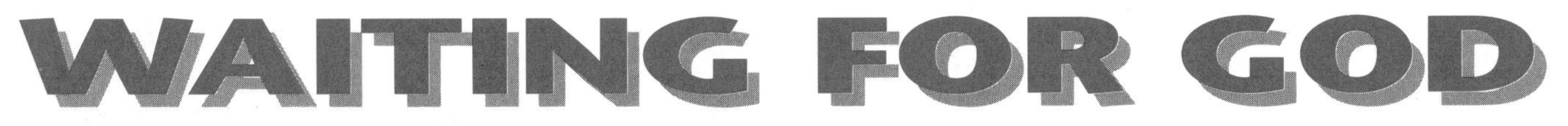

# WAITING FOR GOD

**HOLLY** brings on board an unidentified object. Rimmer thinks it might contain 'Quagaars', a race of aliens with green hair and six breasts. But it turns out to be nothing more than "a smegging garbage pod!" Lister, meanwhile, is obsessed by the history of cats, as he discovers an old cat church - and priest - aboard the ship. It turns out he is the Cat People's God - and also the person indirectly responsible for most of their deaths. If only he could have explained that what they thought was a star chart was in fact his dirty laundry list. ■

# CONFIDENCE & PARANOIA

**LISTER** catches a mutated pneumonia virus and starts feverishly hallucinating. He creates two characters in his mind: Confidence and Paranoia. While Confidence encourages Lister to find Kochanski's hologram disc, Paranoia sides with Rimmer in dragging him down. But both Confidence and Paranoia are killed, and instead of Kochanski appearing from her disc, the unthinkable happens: a second hologram of Rimmer materialises. ■

# ME$^2$

**NOW THERE** are two Rimmers on board - double trouble for Lister. The original Rimmer moves out to share a room with his double and leaves behind a video of his own death, causing Lister to ponder his final words - "Gazpacho soup!". But Lister is sidetracked when Holly tells him of the imminent arrival of the Norweb Federation, intent on obtaining payment for the electricity used by the light Lister left on in his bathroom over 3,000,000 years ago. Meanwhile, the Rimmers aren't getting on - and the spaceship ain't big enough for the both of them. ■

H

RED
DWARF
SEASON TWO

# KRYTEN

*"There's a perfectly logical explanation for everything - with the possible exception of Little Jimmy Osmond."*

*- Holly*

**RED DWARF** receives a distress call from the crashed spaceship Nova 5. As usual, Rimmer fears this means aliens. But according to Nova 5's box-headed 'service mechanoid', Kryten, the ship contains lifeforms of a much less hostile nature - women. The three Red Dwarf crew men boldly spruce themselves up to respond to the call. But when they arrive at the scene, it is clear that Jane, Tracy and Anne are dead and have been for centuries. But what will Kryten do now? After all, he is programmed to wait on the human race (as he explains, "I serve, therefore I am"). In the end, Lister takes pity on him and brings Kryten back to live with them. ■

# BETTER THAN LIFE

**THE POST** pod arrives - 3 million years late, which is about average for second class mail. It contains a video game called Better Than Life, which plugs into the brain and allows the player to experience his or her fantasies. The Cat proceeds to get himself two girlfriends - Marilyn Monroe and a mermaid (top half fish, bottom half woman). But Rimmer can't control his imagination, and ends up with a wife, seven kids, a mortgage and an unsympathetic Outland Revenue Collector. This continues until the others find themselves caught up in his nightmare - buried up to their necks in sand, smeared with jam and about to be eaten by ants. It comes as a relief to everyone when the game ends. ■

# THANKS FOR THE MEMORY

**LISTER WAKES** up to find that his leg has been mysteriously broken and that somebody has completed his prized jigsaw. It turns out that the memories of the crew over the past four days have been erased. But by whom? And why? Meanwhile, Lister feels sorry for Rimmer and, as a 'death day' present, decides to give him the memory of an affair that he had with one Lise Yates. Although all goes well to begin with, Rimmer becomes increasingly troubled. Discovering Lise's letters to Lister, Rimmer realises he's been duped and forces Lister to come clean. Only when Lister watches the replay of the past four days' events on the trusty Black Box is he able to make sense of his broken leg. ■

# STASIS LEAK

**A LEAK FROM** the suspended animation chamber creates a doorway to the past. Lister immediately assumes that this is the best way back to Christine Kochanski, while Rimmer sees it as a chance to save his own life. But things don't go to plan: Lister is late for his own wedding; Rimmer can't convince himself that he's a hologram; and when three Rimmers, three Listers and three Cats appear in the same room, things get a bit complicated.... ■

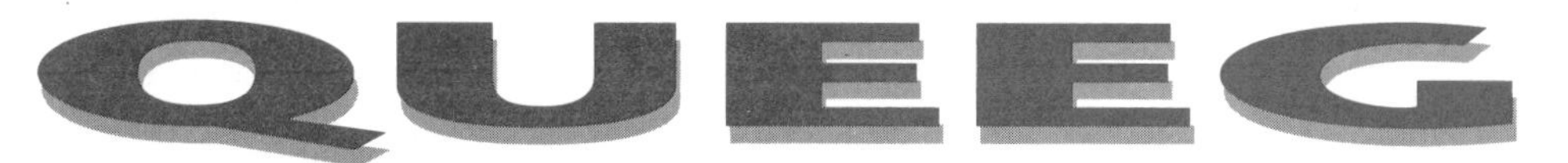

# QUEEG

**HOLLY'S PERFORMANCE** is on the decline. Does he get all his information from *The Junior Encyclopaedia of Space*? The Red Dwarf back-up computer, Queeg 500, suspects so and takes over the ship, demoting Holly to night watchman. But Queeg's new régime of early mornings, exercise and exams is not a big hit with the crew. Holly is sorely missed, and so plans a comeback. He challenges Queeg to a duel: to the winner, command of Red Dwarf; to the loser, erasure. But all is not what it seems, and it transpires that all of this was Holly's idea of a joke - much to the crew's annoyance. ■

# PARALLEL UNIVERSE

**HOLLY DEVISES** a faster-than-light drive (a box with 'stop' and 'start' buttons) which immediately goes wrong and propels Red Dwarf into a parallel universe. Here, women are the masters and 'masculinists' are fighting for equal rights. Lister, Rimmer and even Holly have female equivalents - while the Cat's counterpart is a dog. Predictably, Lister ends up in bed with his parallel partner, Deb. The trouble is, in this universe the men have the babies - and the Listers didn't take any precautions. Rimmer naturally finds the fact that Lister might be pregnant highly amusing. ■

*"I've never been this near to women before: it makes me want to do something. I don't know what it is, but whatever it is, I want to do a lot of it!"*

- Cat

H

# SEASON THREE

# BACKWARDS

*"A masked man with a sawn-off shotgun sucked bullets out of two cashiers and a security guard in a south London bank tomorrow."*

**KRYTEN** takes his driving test in Starbug 1, one of the mini-spaceships housed within Red Dwarf, but strands himself and Rimmer on the other side of a time-hole (his only reaction: "I suppose you're going to fail me for this....").

Lister and Cat go to the rescue and eventually find their colleagues on a version of twentieth century Earth. But despite Lister's initial joy at being home, there is a problem: on this Earth time runs backwards.

Here, people take money from busker's hats, and cafés are populated by customers who spit tea back into teacups and messily disgorge chocolate eclairs. Newspapers report events that have yet to happen, and offer job vacancies that offer good prospects of demotion. However, there aren't many openings for a dead hologram and an android with a head shaped like a novelty condom.

In order to make a living, Rimmer and Kryten form a night-club double act called The Sensational Reverse Brothers and wow audiences by performing song-and-dance routines and eating boiled eggs 'forwards'.

They plan to stay on the planet and become megastars, but are thwarted by a fistfight that Lister is about to start. Or is that finish? ■

*"Are you saying I've got a big bum?"*

- Lister

*"Big? It's like two badly parked Volkswagens."*

- Rimmer

# MAROONED

**AS RED** Dwarf heads on a collision course for five - count them - black holes, it's time to abandon ship. Lister and Rimmer make their getaway in Starbug, but as Rimmer regales Lister with tales of his military interests (he reveals that in a previous life he was Alexander the Great's chief eunuch), the craft is struck by a meteor and crash lands on an icy planet.

In these conditions, rescuers could be ten feet away and still not find them. Rimmer may not need food to survive, but for Lister three water biscuits, half a bag of soggy smokey bacon crisps, a brown lemon, a tube of bongela gum ointment, a pot noodle and a tin of dogfood is hardly enough.

As time drags on, so the two men see a side to each other neither had thought existed. As personal stories are swapped (Lister lost his virginity on a golf course without even being a club member), Lister makes the magnanimous gesture of throwing his beloved guitar on the fire. Only it's not his guitar, it's part of Rimmer's prized antique Javanese trunk... and when Kryten and Cat eventually come to the rescue, old animosities are reignited. ■

# POLYMORPH

*"One swift knee in the happy sacks, and it'll go down like anyone else!"*

- Lister

**A CHAMELEON-LIKE** mutant gets loose aboard Red Dwarf. It is the Ultimate Warrior, according to Holly, a man-made genetic experiment that went wrong. It can acquire energy from negative emotions and change its shape at will to become anything from a cuddly bunny to a beach ball to a monster with more teeth than the entire Osmond family.

One by one, it tracks down the crew of the ship, taking fear from Lister, vanity from the Cat, guilt from Kryten and anger from Rimmer. The crew, though emotionally crippled, decide to "smeg it into oblivion", and the scene is set for a spectacular *Aliens*-style confrontation.

But they can't even decide on a name for their action group (The Committee for the Liberation and Integration of Terrifying Organisms and Their Rehabilitation into Society never really catches on), and the heatseeking bazooka balls chase the Cat instead of the monster. In the final showdown the beast seemingly gets blasted into pieces - or does it? ■

# TIMESLIDES

**KRYTEN** accidentally creates a chemical that can make photographs come to life. The same thing is possible with slides, and soon the crew are stepping into photographs - and back in time. The only caveat is that they can't move outside the borders of the original photo. Cue much merry-making as they run amok through history, blithely ignoring the laws of causality.

Realising that they can change their pasts, and therefore their presents, they begin to experiment. Lister has been fascinated by the gimmick of the Tension Sheet (a simple device made out of plastic bubbles designed to relieve stress), which was invented by Rimmer's high-school room-mate, 'Thicky' Holden, and which earned him a fortune. So now, finding an old photo of himself aged seventeen, and with big bucks in mind, Lister steps back in time and imparts the secret of the Sheet to his youthful self.

So it comes to pass that Lister becomes a millionaire and has to endure regular sex with the delightful Lady Sabrina Mulholland-Jjones. Rimmer can't stand too much of this, and takes it upon himself to restore the time-lines to normal. And what better way to do so than to travel even further back in time and give the secret of the Tension Sheet to himself. ■

# BODYSWAP

**A SKUTTER** (service droid) goes crazy and rewires all the ship's circuitry, producing 2,000 wiring faults and making the whole ship a gigantic booby trap. So when Lister orders a burger and a crispy bar from one of the snack machines, he inadvertently triggers off the ship's self destruct countdown. The only way to defuse the bomb is to transfer the mind of a long-dead female officer into Lister's body, so that she can vocally activate the shut-down mechanism. Unfortunately Holly neglects to tell anyone that the ship no longer has a bomb.

That gives Rimmer ideas: he strikes a deal with Lister to temporarily swop bodies - enabling Rimmer to experience a 'real' body for a change, and in return help Lister to get fit and lose a few pounds of excess flab.

The only trouble is that Rimmer enjoys his new form so much that he treats his body like smeg, pigging out on the food that Kryten prepares for him, his first taste in 3,000,002 years and refuses to reverse the deal.

The only contribution Rimmer has made to Lister's body is to give it breasts. Lister not surprisingly demands his body back, so Rimmer forces Kryten to chloroform Lister. So now Rimmer is again inhabiting Lister's body and has escaped in Starbug, with the others in hot pursuit... ■

# THE LAST DAY

**KRYTEN** discovers his built-in expiry date is almost up and his in-built shut-down chip will automatically activate in twenty-four hours time. He must use his last day to put his affairs in order, dismantle his body and put himself back in his original packing case.

While the mechanoid has been programmed to accept oblivion, Lister feels sorry for him and embarks on a scathing attack on organised religion. Rimmer reveals hitherto untold emotional depths, confessing that his parents were Seventh Day Advent Hoppists - due to a misprint in their Bible they used to hop every Sunday.

As Kryten prepares to meet his maker, the other crew members determine to make his final day the best of his life. No easy task for someone whose idea of fun is to go to the laundry room and fold sheets. Nevertheless, Lister is determined Kryten's going to enjoy his time in a profitless and non-practical way. He even goes to the trouble of building the robotic Marilyn Monroe kit that's been hanging around the ship for years, whilst Holly knocks up a special android home brew using Vimto and liquid nitrogen.

For the first time, Kryten experiences true pleasure, complete with hangover - and decides that he'd much rather delay his departure. He can override his shutdown programme, but the catch is that his replacement mechanoid comes fitted with instructions to kill its predecessor if necessary. But Lister, Rimmer and Cat won't let him down and square up to the formidable Robocop-style visitor, Hudzen, in a spectacular battle on the landing gantry. ■

*"There's no such thing as Silicon Heaven."*

- Lister

*"Then where do all the calculators go?"*

- Kryten

RED DWARF
SEASON FOUR

*"I thought it was a bit too strange - actually meeting someone who didn't want to vomit all over me in complete loathing."*

A **VALENTINE'S** Day special. Kryten rescues a female droid, Camille, from a crashed vessel. She, like him, is a 4000-series, but a GTi model with realistic toes and a slide-back sunroof head. Predictably, Kryten finds himself falling in advanced mutual compatibility on the basis of a primary initial indent - what humans call 'love at first sight'.

When Rimmer sees her, his reaction is the same - he perceives her as a beautiful hologram. When they get back to base, Lister sees her as the last human woman left alive (and a very attractive one at that), and makes plans to start rebuilding the human race. But soon it transpires that Camille is a Pleasure GELF, a Genetically Engineered Life Form, who appears to each individual as their perfect companion. (The Cat is not at all disappointed to find that his perfect companion is none other than himself.)

# CAMILLE

Initially, Kryten is upset and curses the fact that the course of true advanced mutual compatibility never runs in a glitch bug-free way. However, when Camille reveals her natural form as a slimy green blob with tentacles, Kryten confesses that he still finds her attractive - and he's programmed not to lie. They spend an enchanted evening together, dining and dancing at Parrots Restaurant on G-Deck. But it can't last: Camille's still-besotted husband Hector arrives, a fellow blob she had left several years ago but who never gave up looking for her. In a touching *Casablanca*-like finale, Kryten tells her she'll regret it if she stays and stoically waves goodbye... ■

*"What's so great about being human?"*

- Lister:

*"Listy, don't knock it till you've tried it..."*

- Rimmer:

# DNA

**THE RED DWARF** crew board an unidentified derelict craft and are horrified to come across a skeleton with three heads. Rimmer is convinced that they've discovered *Thing*-like aliens. But in fact, it is the result of an accident with a strange machine aboard the ship - a DNA Modifier that can transform living things by restructuring their DNA .

Lister is accidentally turned into a chicken by the Cat, and then into a hamster by a well-meaning Kryten. Meanwhile, Kryten himself is inadvertently made human and starts to enjoy his flesh-and-blood form - despite now having no zoom-function in his eyes, his nipples not working and his having a particularly ugly appendage. Being human soon loses its charm and, having insulted his own spare heads, Kryten decides to revert to his old self.

There remains the problem of the rampaging curry monster - the result of Lister's leftovers having fallen into the machine. Fortunately, there is a secret weapon - lager, the only thing that can kill a vindaloo. ■

# JUSTICE

> *"Trust me - my whole case hinges on proving you're a dork."*
>
> - Defence Lawyer Kryten

**RED DWARF** picks up an escape pod from a prison ship. But what's inside? It could either be beautiful prison guard Barbara Bellini or a psychotic mass-murdering Simulant.

The Dwarf crew have to satisfy their curiosity, but are taking no chances: they take the pod to a penal colony called Justice World, where there are facilities to deal with the Simulant if the worst comes to the worst.

To enter Justice World, the crew first have to pass a test in order to get past the guilt-detecting mind-probe. Kryten and the Cat just about pass, and so does Lister - despite a bit of 'car scrumping' when he was young.

But the hapless Rimmer is found guilty of the second degree murder of the crew of Red Dwarf and, with the aid of locking metal punishment boots, is sent to the Justice Zone for 9,000 years.

Here, any attempted crime is immediately inflicted upon the transgressor - a form of instant justice. Meanwhile, the pod has opened and the occupant is definitely not Barbara Bellini... ■

# WHITE HOLE

*"If we miss, we're going to get a planet in the face."*

**- Rimmer**

**KRYTEN** mends the talking toaster by means of a process called 'intelligence compression'. Having perfected the technique, he can now get to work on curing Holly's computer-senility and restore her to genius-level. But something goes wrong: Holly's intelligence shoots up to 12,000, whilst her lifespan is exponentially reduced. She now has only three minutes to live and so shuts herself down to conserve energy. In so doing, the ship's power is cut, leaving the crew trapped.

They use Kryten as a battering-ram to get through fifty-three metal doors, but then discover that time is doing strange things. The cause is a nearby white hole, towards which the ship is helplessly drifting. As Kryten explains, this is a very rare spacial phenomenon - for each action there is an equal and opposite reaction, and whereas black holes suck matter from the universe, white holes spew time back into it.

Rimmer declares that he will not sacrifice himself to save the crew, but luckily the briefly reactivated Holly has a plan. A thermonuclear device will be fired at a nearby sun in order to catapult a planet into the mouth of the white hole and close it up. However, Lister is not happy with Holly's calculations and, after a vote, he is elected to use his pool playing skills to fire the bomb to its correct destination. But nobody was quite expecting the trick-shot that Lister had in mind... ■

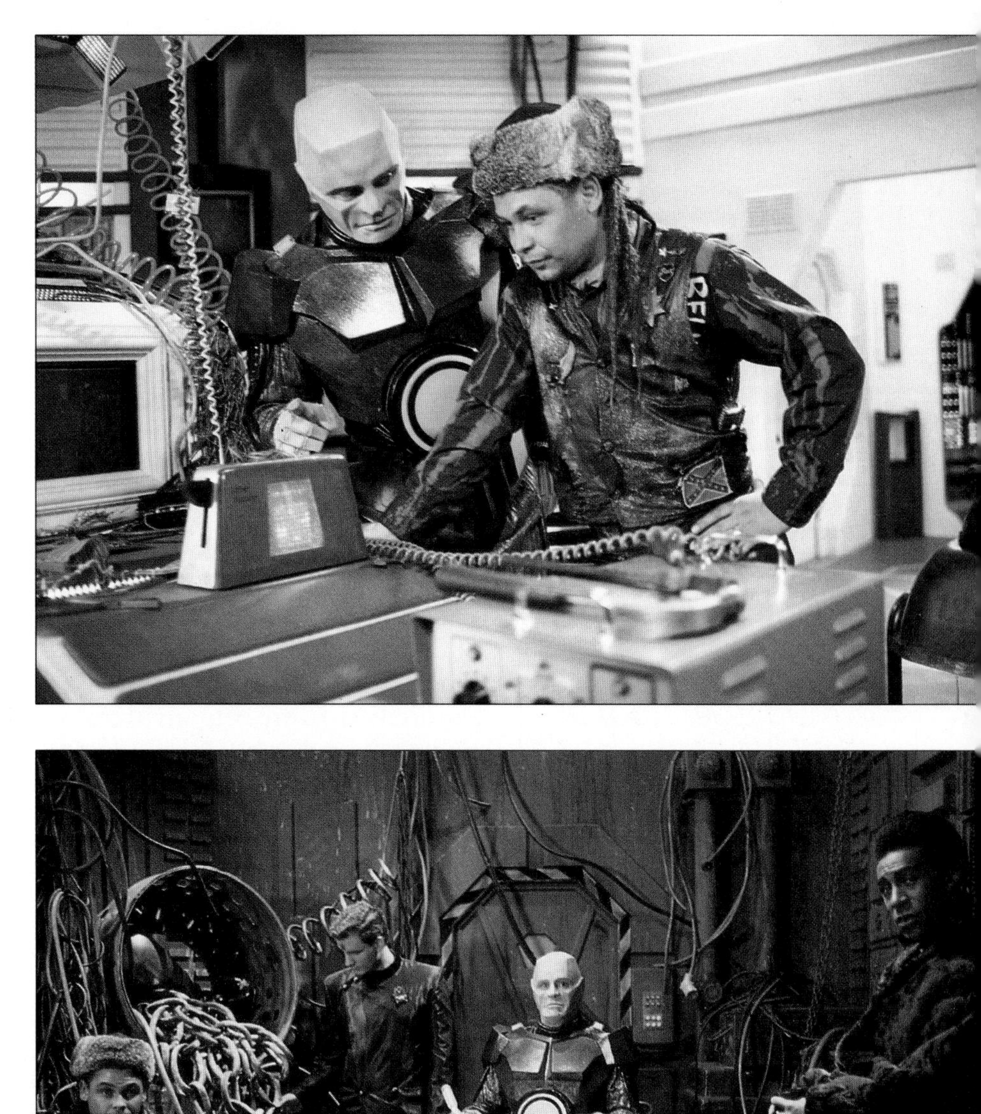

# DIMENSION JUMP

*"Smoke me a kipper, I'll be back for breakfast!"*
- Ace

**IN A PARALLEL** universe, another Arnold Rimmer exists. Commander 'Ace' Rimmer is a test pilot in the Space Corps: he is charming, intelligent, popular, brave and modest. Being the heroic type, he jumps at the chance to test-fly a dimension-jumping prototype spacecraft and, after breaking the 'speed of reality', crosses into Red Dwarf's dimension - crashing into Starbug in the process.

Starbug crash-lands on a water-planet, but Ace does not desert them and follows down to help. Aboard the Starbug he comes face-to-face with his counterpart Rimmer and an instant mutual dislike develops. Despite Ace's broken arm, he and Lister brave the elements to fix the craft.

After this spectacular display of courage, the rest of the crew think he's quite a guy - except the original Rimmer, who suggests that Ace has "greased his way up the old boy network, towel-flicked his way into the Space Corps, mason's handshook his way into flight school and brown-tongued his way up the ranks".

Meanwhile, the Cat has a broken leg, sustained during Starbug's crash, and is becoming delirious - hallucinating about anoraks with furry collars and suits worn with cardigans. Once aboard Red Dwarf again, Ace says he can patch-up the Cat with a bit of micro-surgery, but that afterwards he must move on. He can stand his spineless counterpart no longer ("the man's a maggot") and there are a billion other realities to explore... ■

**KRYTEN** discovers a strange device in the research lab of Red Dwarf. It can convert an individual into digital information and then transmit him in the form of light beams to another point in space. The crew decide to explore the nearest planet with breathable air, thousands of light years away.

Rimmer and Kryten go first, but are chased by two Godzilla-like dinosaurs and taken prisoner by a gun-toting Elvis Presley. Lister and the Cat follow and are captured by Hitler. While in jail they are interrogated by the Roman Emperor Caligula and witness the execution of Winnie the Pooh by a firing squad consisting of Al Capone, Mussolini, Richard III and... James Last. It's clear that something very strange is going on.

# MELTDOWN

Kryten deduces that they have been transported to a huge wax-droid theme park. The good droids are involved in a gruesome *Westworld*-type war with the evil droids - and the baddies are winning. Rimmer sees it as his destiny to lead to victory those goodies that remain - a motley crew including Albert Einstein, Marilyn Monroe and Stan Laurel.

A huge battle ensues and, thanks to a suicide mission by Queen Victoria, the goodies win. Rimmer returns to base to celebrate Victory in Wax-world Day, but has no conscience about wiping out the entire population of the planet. Lister is disgusted by the pointlessness of it all, and devises his own vile punishment for Rimmer... ■

*"Rasputin, bring in the bucket of soapy frogs and remove his trousers!"*

**- The Emperor Caligula**

RED
DWARF
SEASON FIVE

"If I gave the order, those guys would crawl on their bellies on broken glass with their flies unzipped..."

- Rimmer

**STARBUG** comes into contact with another craft that doesn't show up on the monitors. It is a Holoship called Enlightenment, consisting of a vessel and crew that are entirely computer-generated holograms. What is more, the crew are holograms of Space Corps elite personnel.

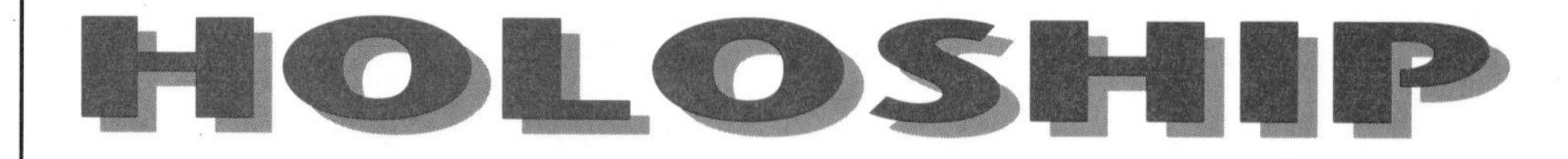

# HOLOSHIP

Rimmer is convinced that the Holoship is his true spiritual home: the fact that the ship's regulations impose sex twice a day with the lovely Nirvanah Crane is an added bonus. But he faces one problem: Enlightenment already has a full crew and new members can only join on a dead-man's-shoes basis.

To gain a place, Rimmer has to challenge an existing member to an intelligence contest: the loser will forfeit his or her life. Rimmer makes plans to cheat, but his competitor withdraws from the contest and Rimmer is then assigned a place. Rimmer heads for his new home - only to discover that his new-found love, Nirvanah Crane, has sacrificed her life for him.

Rimmer now has to choose whether to fulfil his career dreams. Against the odds, Rimmer returns to Red Dwarf, explaining, "Nirvanah and I will not be apart - we just won't be together". Aaaah... ■

"My mother was a bitch queen from hell."

- Rimmer

# INQUISITOR

**THE INQUISITOR,** a fearsome Darth Vader-lookalike Simulant, roams through time weeding out life's wastrels and erasing the worthless. Naturally, the Red Dwarf crew are in big trouble.

But as each crew member comes up for judgement, Rimmer surprisingly makes it through; so too does the Cat. But Kryten and Lister are not so fortunate - they both had the potential to make something of themselves, but failed to do so. Kryten is programmed to live unselfishly, and so his good works derive not from fine motives but from his digital command-programme; meanwhile, Lister's response to questioning is a somewhat unhelpful "spin on it!".

Before the Inquisitor can blast them into oblivion with his power-glove, a double of Kryten arrives from the future to rescue them. The Inquisitor, however, has altered the time-lines and created replacements for the two escapees. Thus, when Kryten and Lister make contact with their old shipmates, they're unrecognised and given a hostile reception.

All is not lost, however, and with the Inquisitor's stolen power-glove and a secret password from Kryten's future incarnation ('enig'), Lister manages to save the day. ■

Unspeakable One - the physical embodiment of his self-loathing. They try to save him, but the bazookoids have little effect. Eventually the beast disappears and they take Rimmer back to the Starbug.

Here, Lister, Kryten and Cat decide that the only way to escape is to make Rimmer feel good about himself, persuading him that they really like him. This is no easy task, but with a little *Iron John*-style male bonding and a lot of gushing compliments, Rimmer's self-esteem slowly begins to return. Thus Starbug is able to lift-off. On the way home, Rimmer asks his shipmates if they meant all they'd previously said. The answer is unanimously negative. ■

# TERRORFORM

**"This is one weird place - strange animal noises, unbearable stench, squelchy underfoot - just like your laundry basket at the end of the month!"**

**- The Cat to Lister**

**KRYTEN** and Rimmer go moon-hopping in the Starbug, but run into trouble on one particular moon when Rimmer is abducted and Kryten sustains fearful injuries as the landscape starts to reform itself. Back aboard Red Dwarf, Kryten is patched-up by Lister and tells his story.

Lister, the Cat and Kryten return to the moon, and discover it is an artificial planetoid that can tune into an individual's psyche and adapt its terrain to mimic his mental state. In this instance, it has reconfigured itself using Rimmer's subconscious as a template. In other words, they have landed inside Rimmer's mind. Here, all Rimmer's personal demons are made flesh - and there are quite a few of them.

After crossing the Swamp of Despair and traversing the Wood of Humiliation, they discover Rimmer in a dungeon about to be tortured by a huge slimy beast called The

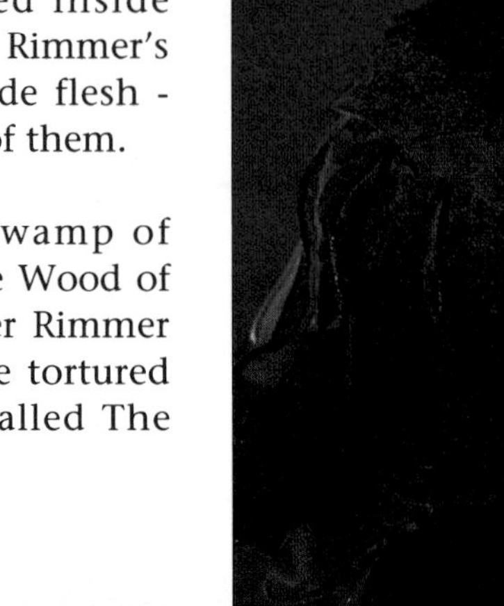

**THE CREW** take Starbug to visit an arctic planet, where they discover a Viral Research Centre. A sign tells them they are in 'most gross danger', a fact they start believing on encountering a hologram of a mad scientist, Dr Lanstrom.

She has contracted an awful holo-virus, which gives her the power to kill with death-rays from her eyes. The crew escape from Dr Lanstrom - but have they escaped from the virus? Rimmer takes no chances and commits the others to three months in quarantine.

There, in Bay 47, nothing gets in and nothing gets out, not even a molecule. The only things the internees have to entertain them are a knitting magazine and a video entitled *Wallpapering, Painting and Stippling - a DIY Guide*.

Predictably, Lister, Kryten and Cat soon start getting on each other's nerves - much to Rimmer's delight. But there's no sign of any virus. That is until one day Rimmer appears dressed in a red and white checked dress, ranting about 'the potato king': it's clear he's been contaminated and has gone completely loopy.

He tries to sentence the others to two hours W.O.O. (With Out Oxygen), but they manage to escape. A showdown is inevitable: Lister, Kryten and the Cat versus a mad transvestite Rimmer and his friend Mr Flibble, a malevolent glove-puppet... ■

# QUARANTINE

**KRYTEN** and Lister inadvertently create a Triplicator that can triplicate anything, combining the best elements of the subject in one copy and the worst in the other. For example, when they try it on a strawberry, one copy tastes delicious, whereas the other is riddled with maggots.

However, when they attempt to reverse the process, it leads to disaster and Red Dwarf starts to explode. The crew race for the Starbug and only just escape with their lives when Red Dwarf is blown into tiny pieces. Fortunately, the Triplicator has created two other Red Dwarfs. Starbug lands on the first and the crew is greeted by alternative versions of themselves embodying the best parts of their personalities. These are the 'highs', who spend their time philosophising, reading poetry and trying to improve their minds. Everything on the ship is divine - even the pot noodles.

But there is another ship, crewed by the 'lows', who represent the evil parts of their vessel. They capture Lister (who unwisely informs them they are two lettuces short of an allotment) and impregnate him with a device enabling them to dictate his actions by remote control. He is made to attack his shipmates and the ensuing violence is only stemmed when Lister is chloroformed by Kryten.

# DEMONS & ANGELS

*"Abandon shop!"*

*"This is not a daffodil!"*

- Holly

Having seen off the danger, they collect the Triplicator and reverse-the-reversal, bringing the situation back to the point before Red Dwarf blew up in the first place. But the Cat still has the remote control and intends having some fun... ■

*"He thinks we're either a threat, food or a mate. He's gonna either kill us, eat us or hump us!"*
- Lister

# BACK TO REALITY

**THE RED DWARF** team go underwater to investigate the SSS Esperanto, whose crew have all committed suicide - and so have all the marine creatures, bar one. The cause is a giant squid that squirts ink, inducing hallucinations and despair.

The Starbug takes off for cover and promptly crashes. The crew 'wake up' to discover that for four years they have been playing a sophisticated video game called Red Dwarf. They are disorientated at first, gradually discover that Kryten is really macho detective called Jake Bullett; the Cat is Duane Dibbly (a dork who wears nylon shirts and anoraks); Lister is a fascist politician; and Rimmer is a down-and-out.

Kryten/Jake Bullett kills a human and all four game-players reach the point of committing suicide. But at the last minute, they find out they've been having a group hallucination, caused by the giant squid's inking. Holly, meanwhile, has blown up the beast. ■

**WITH *RED*** *Dwarf*, Rob Grant and Doug Naylor were attempting to meld two genres, comedy and science fiction, that don't instinctively work together. "What we wanted to do," says Rob, "was a comedy with no cardigans and no formica. Some-thing that was a bit different. *Steptoe and Son* in space". Unfortunately, the powers that be had a little difficulty grasping the concept, despite it already having had a dry run as 'Dave Hollin - Space Cadet' on Rob and Doug's Radio 4 comedy show, *Son of Cliché*.

Doug takes up the story: "Originally, we sent the pilot script off to Paul Jackson, who we'd worked with on *Carrott's Lib* and *Three of a Kind*, and John Lloyd, who'd brought us in as head writers on *Spitting Image*. They both really liked it, and there was even talk of them making it as a co-production. We expected it to be made within months. But when Paul took it to the BBC, it was rejected. In all, it was rejected three times. He kept taking it back and saying, 'Are you sure you've read it? This is something different.' And they kept saying, 'Yes, we have. Go away.'

"All along we'd felt it was absolutely critical that the show was made for the BBC. We felt the

**Above:** *Typical comic invention: curry in a human form in 'D.N.A.'* **Right:** *Norman Lovett (the first Holly), complete with legs, studies the model set.*

# Rob Grant & Doug Naylor

# SCRIPTS

## "Steptoe and Son in space"

**Above:** *Doug Naylor, Ed Bye, director of seasons 1-4, and Rob Grant.*

extra five minutes you got from not having ad breaks was essential to tell more complex stories and establish a deeper sense of characterisation. And at the time, our opinion of ITV comedies was unprintable. So even when they rejected us, we refused to concede defeat. We even turned down the opportunity to turn it into a movie for Film on Four. Worst case, we thought, was we'd wait until they all retired or died and resubmit it.

"Finally, we decided to go and see the Head of Comedy and try to change his mind. He was wearing white shoes and grey slacks, and instantly we knew we were in trouble.

"'Well, I've read the script,' he said charmingly, 'and I don't like it. What's more, I've given it to all the producers in the comedy department...' Our minds backtracked to the series of photographs of BBC comedy stars that lined the corridor. Molly Sugden. John Inman. '...and none of us like it.'

"The sticking point seemed to be that the show was set on a space ship. No-one, he contended, could relate to people who live on a space ship. Bizarrely, he suggested the public would be more comfortable if the opening shot were to feature people sitting on a sofa; we could then pull back to reveal a set of French windows, and then somehow this all turns out to be set on a space ship.

"We pointed out that, on the whole, spaceships didn't have French windows. 'And that's your problem,' he countered. 'You see, the public don't like science fiction.'

"Well, we'd been waiting for this one. So we hit him with the list: 'What about *Star Wars*? What

**Above:** *The success of the show has resulted in bigger budgets for visual effects.*
**Below:** *Kryten and the mechanoid Camille from 'Camille'.*

about *Alien*? *Star Trek*? *Dr Who*? *The Hitchhiker's Guide to the Galaxy*? *E.T.*? *Close Encounters*?' We went on and on. And on.

"There was a long pause. 'You-'re right,' he finally said. 'The public *do* like science fiction, don't they?' And right there and then, he agreed to commission us for a science fiction comedy series - that *wasn't Red Dwarf* ! I think he did it to get us out of his office, otherwise we'd have been there to this day.

"It was a bizarre feeling, when people asked us how the meeting had gone, and we said, 'Terrible. He commissioned us to write a science fiction comedy series.'"

In the early episodes, Rob and Doug were still feeling their way, but over the years they've taken the team out of their environment and, as Rob puts it, put "a bit more oomph into it. A lot of sitcoms just have people sitting round tables and talking. What we do is get an

idea, write it, and then try to make it possible."

Perhaps the biggest dilemma Rob and Doug faced was whether to include a robot. "The problem was finding a new angle," explains Rob. "The first Kryten episode was like C3PO part two." Eventually they came up with the concept of a robot/android that was more integral to the plot.

It's since the arrival of Kryten that the series has really taken off, but Doug Naylor reveals how Robert Llewellyn barely survived his debut: "The first scene was in a sauna. He'd just put his suit and mask on for the very first time. The scene required him to light two candles with his fingers, so he was all wired up for a flame to come out of his fingers. Because it was wet in there and he was sweating, it was backfiring all the time and he was electrocuting himself. So it was day one, it was 120 degrees and every time he moved his arm he got an electric shock. He just couldn't believe what he'd let himself in for. The scene was cut from the show in the end."

One aspect that has made *Red Dwarf* a success, particularly with its younger audience, is the vulgar streaks of humour that cut through the metaphysical concepts. But there is more to the humour than meets the eye. Of all the cast, Craig Charles most appreciates *Red Dwarf's* comic sophistication. "There are no snotty noses and no smelly bums without good reason," says Craig. "There's a lot more subtext to it, the jokes are character-based. The toilet gags are heavily based in the plot." ■

**Above:** *Rob Grant and Robert Llewellyn, in full Kryten make up, during filming on* Red Dwarf.
**Below:** *The Starbug has enabled the show to move to a variety of new locations.*

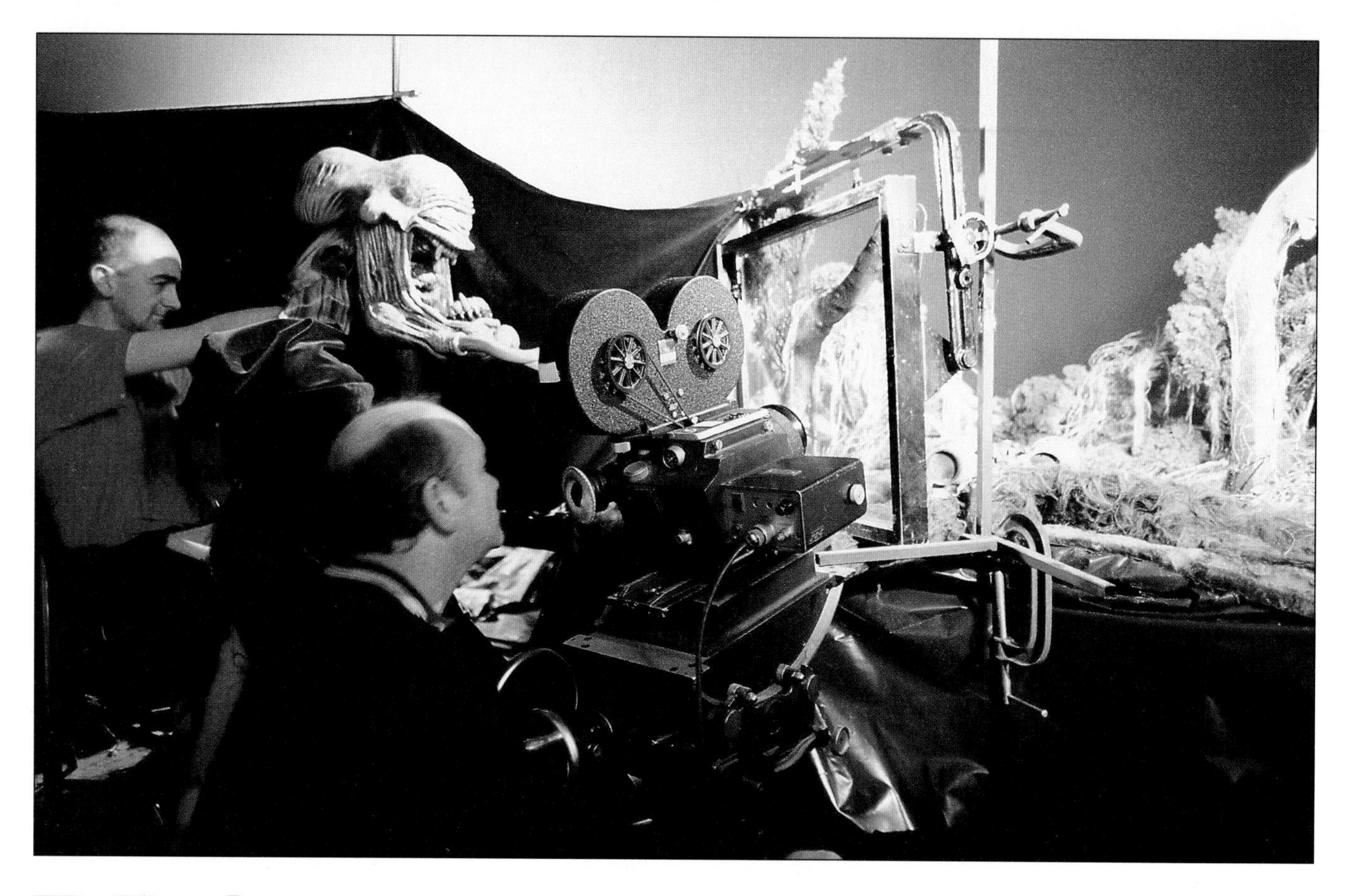

# PRODUCTION

## Paul Jackson

### *"A strangulated birth"*

**IF THERE** is one person who can claim total credit for getting *Red Dwarf* onto television, it is Paul Jackson. Jackson, who had previously been responsible for *The Young Ones* and *Saturday Night Live*, was the man who finally got BBC Northwest to commission *Red Dwarf* back in 1986. Of course, that makes it sound simple. In the world of TV, things are never that simple. Jackson, now the head of Carlton TV, takes up the story.

"Like a lot of these things, it was a strangulated birth, which in the end fell into the right place at

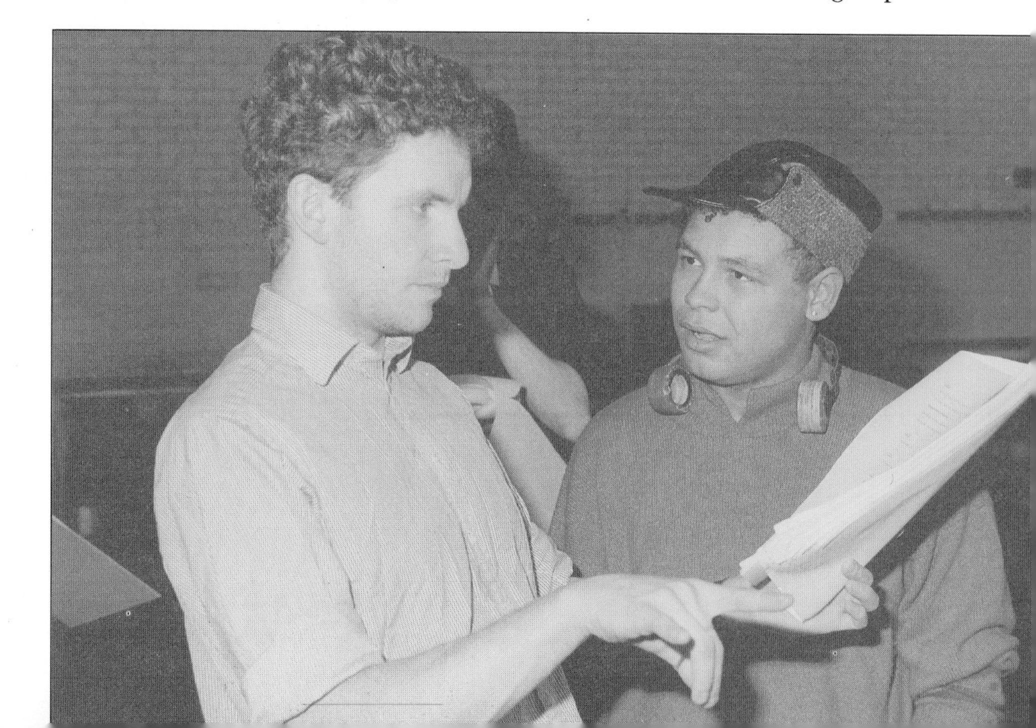

**Above:** *Alien environments can be created in the studio.* **Right:** *Chris Barrie and Craig Charles run through the script.*

the right time. I had done *Happy Families* with Ben Elton in Manchester following *The Young Ones*. The BBC then asked me to try and get more of these off-the-wall projects underway. The way the BBC used to work was that when they did the next year's projections they wrote in returning series, so they had pencilled in *Happy Families 2*, but there was never any intention of doing another series. So there was therefore this amount of money that had been allocated to independent productions with my name on it, so to speak."

This was the mid-eighties, when the BBC was just beginning to commission programmes from outside companies, of which *Red Dwarf* turned out to be among the first. But, as we said, things were not that simple...

"I'd made *Happy Families* as an independent, and now there was this money in the independent allocation which meant that even though *Happy Families 2* wasn't happening, it was hard to bring the money back in-house. So there was quite a momentum going. Meanwhile, I'd been developing projects with Rob and Doug. We hadn't got anywhere with *Red Dwarf* with Gareth Gwenlan at the BBC in London and I remember coming back from Manchester on the train, and it must have been the early days of portable phones because I phoned Rob and Doug up from the train, and I said, 'Look, I think I've got a slot here - can you put *Red Dwarf* into it?' And they said 'Yes, definitely', so we went ahead and got it commissioned on that basis. Then we missed the first series because of the electricians' strike. We kept going in for rehearsals but kept getting knocked back, so eventually we abandoned it for a year."

**Above:** *Chris Barrie as Arnold Rimmer.*
**Left:** *Craig Charles as Dave Lister.*

But Jackson was finally working on a series with his two protégés: "I had always wanted to do something with Rob and Doug, ever since they had worked with

**Right:** *Well-known celebrities join the cast in 'Meltdown'.*
**Below:** *Rimmer and Mr Flibble in 'Quarantine'.*

me on *Three Of A Kind* and *Carrott's Lib*. Eventually they submitted scripts for *Lance Bland, Newshound*, which was a cross between *Bulldog Drummond* and *Casablanca*, and I really didn't like the parody element, I felt it wouldn't have legs. I gave them lots of notes on rewriting it, and typical Rob and Doug, they rewrote it and came back and said, 'Would you mind if it was a space comedy?' To which I replied, 'Why the bloody hell lumber yourself with another problem?' Space comedy had traditionally not worked; you've got all the problems of the visual effects - it looks like *Blake's 7* if you're not careful. And they said, 'Well, if it's funny it would still be alright.' And I said, 'Well, that's true, but why make it more difficult for yourself, because everybody you tell it's going to be a space comedy will have an immediate anti on it, because it's never worked.'" In a way, Jackson still believes he was right. "I think the sci-fi thing did work against it at first. For a long time it limited the audience because it is a real cut-off. To a certain section of the potential audience, it was a case of, 'Oh, it's sci-fi, and I don't like sci-fi.' But with an audience of 7,000,000, I think they've won them over now."

Jackson, however, was won over by the first scripts: "I liked *Red Dwarf* from the very first; I think we struggled a bit for the first six episodes, and we really didn't get bedded-in until the second series, but I think that the relationship between Rimmer and Lister was good, and I thought the idea of the Cat was a brilliant conceit."

Having initially been indifferent to science fiction, Jackson has finally been converted by *Red Dwarf*: "I like the idea that you can use science fiction as a kind of metaphor for society as it is now. It gives you the freedom to write about society in a way that perhaps you don't have in realistic writing.

Look at Martin Amis: I'm sure he didn't nick it from 'Backwards', but *Time's Arrow* has taken the same concept for a classic modern day novel. Ultimately Rimmer and Lister are archetypal human beings. As are Kryten and the Cat, albeit that they are not human beings. Everybody knows somebody like each of the characters."

Grant and Naylor's own production company took over from Paul Jackson Productions for *Red Dwarf IV*, but Jackson continues to play close attention to the show: "I think it has got better year by year. At it's best it uses the freedom you gain from positing an unreal universe. But they don't just use it for cheap laughs. 'Camille', for instance, was just such a beautiful exposition of a love story. The fact that one of the partners was a blob was kind of irrelevant." ■

**Above:** *Danny John-Jules at rehearsals.*
**Left:** *Models for the Camille blob in the workshop.*

## "The icing on the cake"

**Right:** *The 'tramp steamer' look created by Mel Bibby.*
**Below:** *The corridor set from the 'good' Red Dwarf in 'Demons and Angels'.*
**Above far right:** *Red Dwarf's medical lab.*
**Below far right:** *The Red Dwarf crew in the cockpit.*

**THE DIVIDING** line between the jobs carried out by Peter Wragg's visual effects team and Mel Bibby's design department is a gossamer thin one. Peter Wragg was intimately involved in putting together the Starbug and seeing that explosions, flights and action sequences came together. Designer Mel Bibby describes his three-person team's job as dealing with "basically everything structurally on the floor. The ship, the structures you walk into and through, are my domain."

Bibby is another BBC veteran, having notched up twenty years worth of work for Auntie. His background, however, is in comedy rather than sci-fi. During the mid-eighties he worked with Paul Jackson and Ben Elton at BBC Manchester and was, in fact, unable to do the first two series of *Red Dwarf*. Bibby was tied up with, "I shouldn't say this, another Paul Jackson production and the greatest flop we've ever seen, *Morris Minor and the Majors*." Being a great fan of science fiction films, Bibby incorporates some of his biggest influences into *Red Dwarf*. "I have to admit that *Aliens* is my biggest cheat. I think that, of all the science fiction films, was the one that

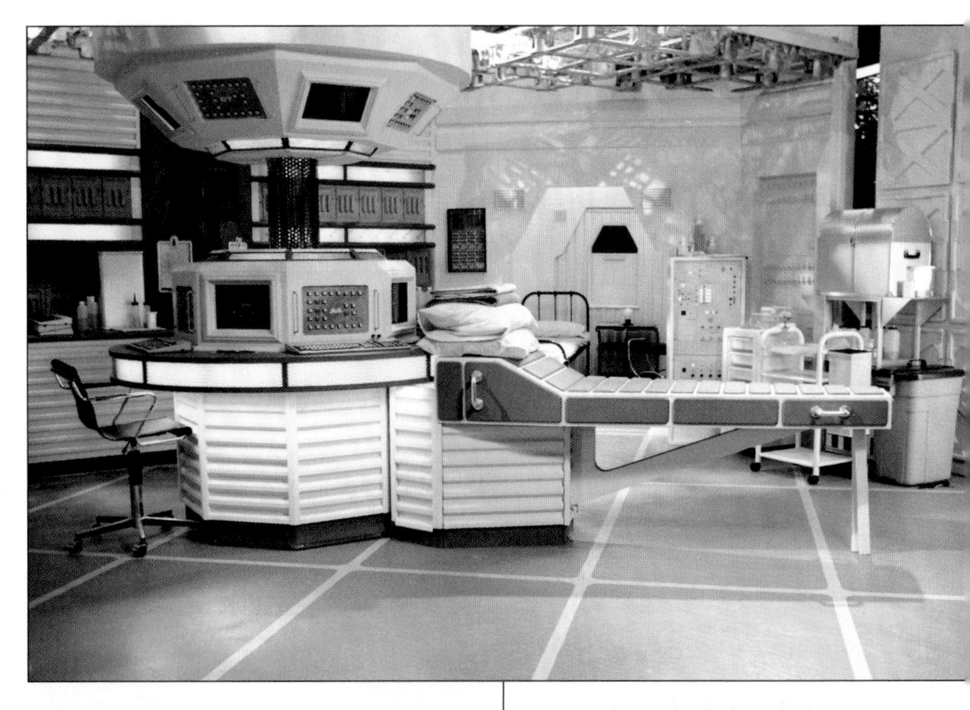

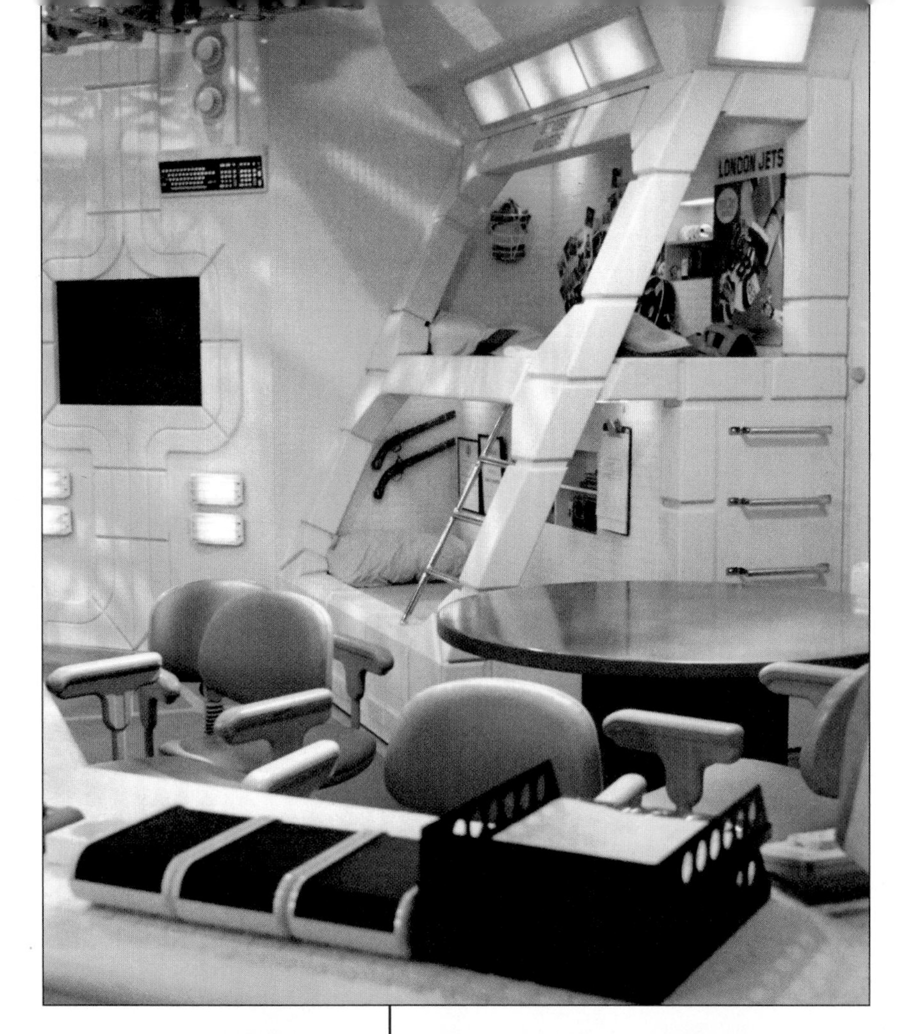


turned around the look. We've gone for a mixture - as did *Aliens* - so when you've got the sleeping quarters it's a smooth look, but the corridors and the guts of the machinery is, as they put it in *Aliens*, a tramp steamer. But that's one of the things about design, there's never anything new - just a progression of various ideas."

The special effects team has a larger budget than the designers, which means that much of the overall look of *Red Dwarf* is down to Mel Bibby's ingenuity. "We often build one set, then after film-

**Left:** *The smooth look of the sleeping quarters.*
**Below:** *An interior set used in 'Back to Reality'.*
**Above right:** *Lister, Kryten and Rimmer in the medical lab.*
**Below right:** *The 'bad' Red Dwarf set in 'Demons and Angels'.*

ing, we rip it apart and reuse it. I remember on *Red Dwarf IV*, when the budget was lower, my assistant and I spent our time robbing the skips in Shepperton and various other stages which were doing commercials, to get materials."

Over the years the sets haven't become more elaborate, but there have been demands for more of them. "The secret is to try and keep it simple," says Bibby. "A lot of it is in the writing. If you notice, they tend to do a lot of close-ups, it's the dialogue that counts. The backing is the icing on the cake."

Despite the film references, shooting *Red Dwarf* in front of a live audience makes the set design more redolent of a theatrical production, with three walls, no roof and a front that is left open so the public can see in.

meant there simply wasn't anywhere to put it. Bibby takes up the story. "With the Starbug, the corridor, the sleeping quarters, plus an audience of 200 people, we only had a cubby hole for the other set. Ed had used one when he worked with Jasper Carrott, so we tried it again on 'Inquisitor'. And afterwards, Ed just said, 'Well, it didn't work on Jasper Carrott and it hasn't worked again!' So we adapted it to look like something else - there's always something you can scrape out of the barrel!"

'Inquisitor' seems to have been the episode where the gremlins took control. There was another scene which involved filming around a lake at night: "The lighting director and his electricians knew where they were putting the lights, but people were walking towards the lights like moths and falling in the water. Well, the lighting director and the electricians were - and they were the ones who were supposed to know where they were placed."

As the designers grew in confidence, Rob and Doug's plots

**Above:** *The impressive set built for 'Justice'.*
**Right:** *The Cat in 'D.N.A.'*

It's a situation that can be frustrating for the designers, who, in aesthetic terms, would rather put together four-sided sets. Bibby concedes that the comedy is *Red Dwarf*'s priority. "The whole point of the exercise is that it is a comedy, and the actors and writers love the audience being there for the inter-reaction. From my purist point-of-view, I don't like them being there, but I can understand how doing it live over one evening gives it that rough edge which makes it so funny." The only time the designers failed to come up with the goods was when director Ed Bye asked for an infinity-perspective set, to give the illusion of distance. Recording live at Shepperton in front of an audience

moved the action around more and more. "I'm really proud of the corridor," adds Bibby. "In *Red Dwarf V* the sleeping quarters were rarely used. They tended to get into the bug or use other sets. Hopefully that's the way it will go in the future. The corridor worked well because it was a good, small set. And it was economically done, using pallets and bits of timber."

It's amazing what a bit of ingenuity can do. A lot of the scenery on *Red Dwarf* originally came from a small plastics factory outside Manchester. "They do things for anybody - Barclays Bank, MOD - and at the beginning of each series, we go and raid them. Most of the corridor was made out of lids for fish tanks. That's the beauty of working on *Red Dwarf*. You're not dealing with a normal sitcom, where there's a lounge, a kitchen, everything else. This is something where anything goes."

With *Red Dwarf* being an independent production for the BBC, everyone involved is more aware of the costs being incurred. They complain about the limitations but, apart from the odd infinity-perspective set, things invariably work out in the end. "Rob and Doug are good to work for, too - if you've got a problem, it ceases to be one once you talk to them. They want the earth, just like everybody else - I mean, I want the earth too, and if we had the money we'd build the earth!" ■

**Below:** *The cockpit on Red Dwarf.*
**Bottom:** *Crossing the swamp in 'Terrorform'.*

# VISUAL EFFECTS

## Peter Wragg

*"I like to think there isn't anything we can't do"*

**Right:** *Starbug, Peter Wragg's finest achievement on* Red Dwarf.
**Below:** *The visual effects team prepare a Starbug shot.*

**THE VISUAL** effects in *Red Dwarf* have taken television science fiction into another dimension. If *Dr Who*'s wobbly TARDIS summed up the first generation of cathode sci-fi, and the formica hell of *Blake's 7* was the second, the intergalactic exploits of the Jupiter Mining Ship Red Dwarf have hit the final frontier.

*Red Dwarf*'s technical trickery encapsulates the best and worst of everything that has already been done. At times it's as slick as a Spielberg movie, at others it's as charmingly rickety as one of *Dr Who*'s Heath-Robinson gadgets.

The man responsible for the visual effects is a veteran of BBC sci-fi, Peter Wragg. He's been with *Red Dwarf* from the start, having already been with the BBC for sixteen years, working on specials like *The Flipside of Dominic Hyde*, and, inevitably, *Dr Who*.

**Above:** *At work on the Red Dwarf model.*

Wragg's childhood ambition was to make models, but "somewhere along the way I was sidetracked and ended up doing the effects." Wragg originally started out at Gerry Anderson's Century 21, working on *Thunderbirds* and *Captain Scarlet* alongside people who later went on to do *Batman*, and brought a wealth of experience to the six-person *Red Dwarf* team.

A total budget of around £200,000 per episode for *Red Dwarf V* sounds like plenty of money, but things are still tight: "It's more than one often gets, but allowing for the amount of effects, it's not that generous. You have to think laterally and tailor what you do to what you've got."

The ideas for the effects are two-way traffic. Rob and Doug go to Peter Wragg with their thoughts, but if he wants to use a certain type of vehicle they often put it in. "The whole experience has been a building process," says Wragg. "Paul Jackson originally said we would need some space shots, then when they were pleased with that it developed into a situation where they said, 'Right, what can you do? Can you do a snow scene or a water situation?'"

As a result of growing confidence, Wragg's work has become more sophisticated and in recent series there have been more external scenes. In the early programmes there were interiors and one or two space scenes, now monsters seem to emerge from every alcove. It's all a hugely enjoyable challenge. "We have a talented team and I like to think that there isn't anything we can't do," says Wragg.

Sometimes they even surprise the writers: "In the early series they wanted the Skutters, which were radio-controlled and which we made as elaborate as we could - much more so than Doug expected at the time. There are always different aspects to achieving effects. When Kryten first appeared we had to decide how to make him look. He's an android but I thought it would be naff to make him metallic, so we made him flesh, but made the flesh angular."

*Red Dwarf* is closer in spirit to *Dr Who* than the original Gerry Anderson shows, since it uses real people instead of puppets, but Peter Wragg believes that *Red Dwarf* is unique. "There just aren't any other comparisons. *Blake's 7* was set in space, but it wasn't fantasy like this is."

One thing Peter Wragg tries to avoid is *Red Dwarf* looking like a cheap imita-

**Right:** *Very fine wire is used for some of the visual effects.*
**Below:** *Starbug caught on the rocks in 'Back to Reality'.*

tion of big budget American space epics. Any similarity between the effects in *Red Dwarf* and *Dark Star* is purely coincidental. "You try to be different every time, but inevitably people have done something similar which you didn't know about. Rob and Doug wanted a lived-in spaceship that wasn't high tech, more run down, so we built on that and made *Red Dwarf* a mining vessel with a meteorite that's crashed into it that's been trundling round space for years."

Effects technology has improved considerably since the *Thunderbirds* days. When Starbug skims over the planet surface and just misses the rocks, wires are still used, but these days they are a lot thinner than the ones that propelled International Rescue. "But it's still a similar process," reveals Wragg. "It's a very fine wire, which is metal and very strong. We find what the limit is in relation to the

**Above:** *A night scene involving a crashed Starbug.*
**Left:** *Setting up a shot for 'Dimension Jump'.*

model and always try to make the models as light as we possibly can."

The fact that *Red Dwarf* has to extract laughs without actually sending up sci-fi lore places a heavy burden on the visual effects team. According to Wragg, "It makes it more difficult, because in order for the comedy to work, the effects have to be believable - while at the same time making it unbelievable, not so convincing that the audience take it too seriously."

Extra credit is due for working to such tight schedules. Filming the effects takes up one of the two days allocated for shooting each episode and then, on the second day, the effects are fed into the plot in front of a live audience. Nerves get frayed but the film gets done. After much thought, Peter Wragg admits to

being particularly gratified by the scenes in *Red Dwarf V* "when Starbug is taking off and things were exploding around it." And all done on a set not much bigger than the average living room.

The Starbug itself is Peter Wragg's greatest achievement. If it looks like a giant insect, that isn't a coincidence: "Rob and Doug called it the White Midget originally. We already had the Blue Midget from earlier, but that wasn't practical because we needed to see people inside. So we revamped it and created another craft. Starbug came from half-ideas. I gave Rob and Doug various drawings and they chose that one." The christening of the ship was fiendishly simple: "It looked like a bug and they said, 'We like the look of that', so they called it Starbug." ■

**Above:** *Ace Rimmer's test ship prepares to land in 'Dimension Jump'.*
**Above left:** *The penal colony, Justice World, from 'Justice'.*
**Far left:** *Various Starbug models in the visual effects workshop.*
**Left:** *Setting up a water tank sequence. The Despair Squid did not appear in the finished programme..*

*"The sky's the limit"*

# Howard Burden

# COSTUME

**RED DWARF** would not be the success it is today without the costumes. Each crew member has developed a distinctive look which perfectly complements their character. The man responsible for the sartorial space-style of the series is Howard Burden, who has worked on *Red Dwarf* since Kryten joined permanently at the beginning of *Red Dwarf III*, and who clothes the entire team.

Burden works closely with Rob, Doug and the director. Between them they talk through the scripts well in advance, to check what is needed. "In an ideal world," says Burden, "I see finished scripts, but then when we are about to start filming they often get an idea for another joke, and they say to me, 'Let's get them in red gingham hats and hobnail boots' and you have three days to get it together. You have to be able to adapt quickly." The tight budget makes it an even

**Above:** *The Cat, Rimmer and Lister.*
**Left:** *The Cavalier costume from 'Terrorform'.*
**Right:** *The Cat in typical flamboyant style.*

greater challenge. Despite looking much more sophisticated, the budget is smaller now than for the first series. "You have to get more ingenious," explains Burden.

Of the main protagonists, Kryten was the first that Burden clothed: "He'd been in that previous episode, but he had to be modified because he had problems in flexibility and movement. At first he was more robotic, but it became obvious that they were going to ask him to do more things, so we had to come up with something more flexible, changing his breast pad and shoulders."

**Right:** *Jane Horrocks as Nirvanah Crane in 'Holoship'.*

**Below left:** *Howard Burden's sketch for the Cavalier costume used in 'Terrorform'.*

**Below right:** *Howard Burden's design for Commander Binks' and Nirvanah Crane's costumes in 'Holoship'.*

One of Burden's main tasks was to tackle the intergalactic crusty, Lister. He was already a scruff of cosmic proportions, but Burden wanted to go further: "Lister's always been a grubby character, beer drinking and dirty. A fat slob basically. He's the only human left on the ship and whatever he has left, he tries to repair it, so everything he's got is deteriotating rapidly. Originally we had him leaving a trail behind him like Linus from Charlie Brown, but we thought that was going a bit far. Instead we gave him a street look, but kept it grubby and smelly."

Rimmer was quite difficult too: "It was a question of getting the military aspect that he would love to have. Because he is pretentious, I put him in a rather starchy tunic and trousers to give him that air of authority. Initially he was in green, but now he's in red because the colours worked better against the Starbug and the interiors which had a lot of dark green. He's more streamlined now."

Burden has succeeded in giving the crew a unique style. Where some might say the storylines and the sets borrow from sci-fi movies and old TV shows, the clothes are definitely original. As Burden says, "It has taken time to establish its own identity, and I want to avoid it looking like *Dr Who* or *Hitchhiker's Guide*."

However, there was a time when Rimmer wore a Captain

Scarlet hat complete with aerial. "That was part of the story," apologises Burden. "He needed to communicate by radio and the aerial had to come out somewhere. It made him look like a prat and he doesn't wear it any more. He wants to be taken more seriously."

If Lister, Rimmer and Kryten demanded outfits in keeping with their space-station, it was the Cat that Howard Burden was able to have most fun with. There had never been anything like the Cat, so Burden's imagination could run riot.

"He is a designer's dream. He's flamboyant, extrovert, and you can go over the top. Like if there's a scene of them all going fishing, everyone's in the proper gear except the Cat, who is in a lamé lurex outfit. He's obsessed with his own looks and you have to go along with that, giving him things like zebra print coats."

Burden's background is in conventional costume design. Many years ago he worked on *Dr Who*, but more recently he has been employed on *The Bill* and *Casualty*. By comparison, *Red Dwarf* is a liberation. Where the brief in those series was for authenticity, he can do anything in *Red Dwarf*. "Exactly. The sky's the limit. What I do is take references and interpret it my own way. It's the job of designers to take ideas and make something new." Sometimes, however, the budget does place restrictions on his department: "It would be impossible to create a *Terminator 2* look for *Red Dwarf*, so it's important instead to make something bright, fresh and fun. The only thing stopping you is your imagination." ■

**Left:** *The Inquisitor costume.*

**Above left:** *Howard Burden's sketch for the Inquisitor's costume.*

**Above right:** *One of the Cat's outrageous costumes designed by Howard Burden.*

# MAKE-UP

## Andria Pennell

*"The make-up has to be funny too"*

**Above:** *The final touches are applied to Craig Charles.*
**Right:** *Chris Barrie in the make-up chair.*

**EVER WONDERED** who gave Craig Charles the space mumps? The answer is Andria Pennell, *Red Dwarf*'s resident make-up genius. Pennell provides the visual ideas to compliment Rob and Doug's words. In the past the crew were fairly simple to make up, but over the years there has been an increasingly heavy workload for the four-person team. In 'Demons and Angels', for instance, Andria Pennell had to make up three different versions of each regular cast member.

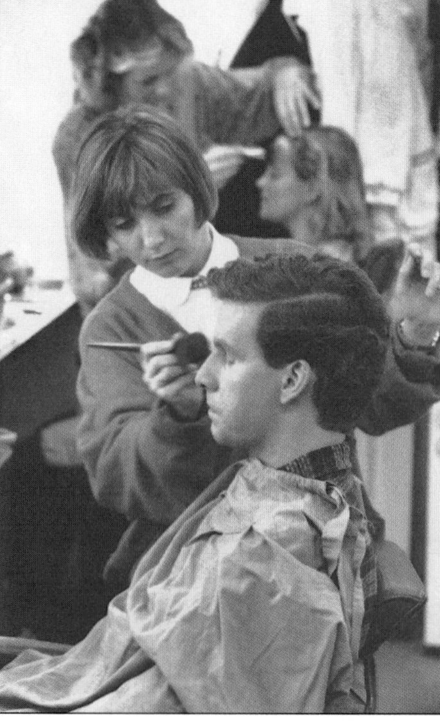

The process begins when Rob and Doug hand her the scripts: "I read what they've done and then I talk to Rob and Doug about what they want, which can be quite wacky to say the least. Then if we are thinking in the same directions, I do it in clay and they look at it and decide if it is funny. If they think it is, I carry on, otherwise I start again."

The biggest problem for make-up was Kryten: "I was brought in because he was having difficulty with his head, and I had worked on prosthetics at Central Television and was able to get the time it took to make him up down from six hours to two hours." Kryten is still a demanding process, though.

"Preproduction for Robert is three weeks, getting the head cast and the pieces made. And we have to do it every three weeks." As with the costume department, the make-up department has to come up with ideas that would never get used on a terrestrial television series. Take Craig Charles' space mumps in 'Justice'. "We took a cast of Craig's head, then sculpted the shape that we wanted the mumps to look like, then started packing it in foam. After a great deal of patience and several goes later, we painted it and shaded it in. The difficult part is making the visuals fit the words - the make-up has to be funny too, and mumps aren't funny. But things are different in space, so you have a bit more licence." ■

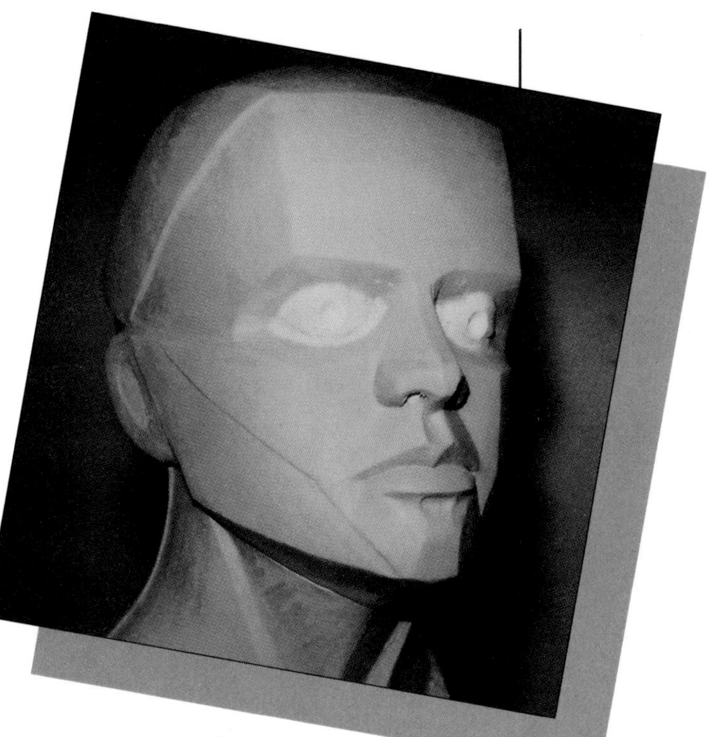

**Above:** *Kryten's head.*
**Below left:** *Robert Llewellyn is transformed into Kryten.*
**Below right:** *'Bad' Lister, one of three Listers made-up for 'Demons and Angels'.*

# THE FUTURE

*"The team head off in directions which TV technology and budgets don't permit"*

**SO WHERE** to next for our intrepid space bums? *Red Dwarf* has been sold all around the world and dubbed into most European languages. The next place to conquer is America. The series has been screened on cable TV and in early 1992 an American pilot was made.

Initially David (*Twin Peaks*) Lynch showed an interest, but eventually Universal Studio produced the one-off and sold it to NBC. Grant and Naylor had turned down previous offers because companies had demanded too many changes ("Americans couldn't take the concept of a dead man in a lead role!" said one potential producer), but inevitably there were some alterations.

The show was recast and only Robert Llewellyn retained his role. Lister became more glamorous, but Rimmer stayed as smeggy as ever despite having a red dot instead of an 'H' on his forehead. According to Rob Grant, this made him look like "Gandhi in space."

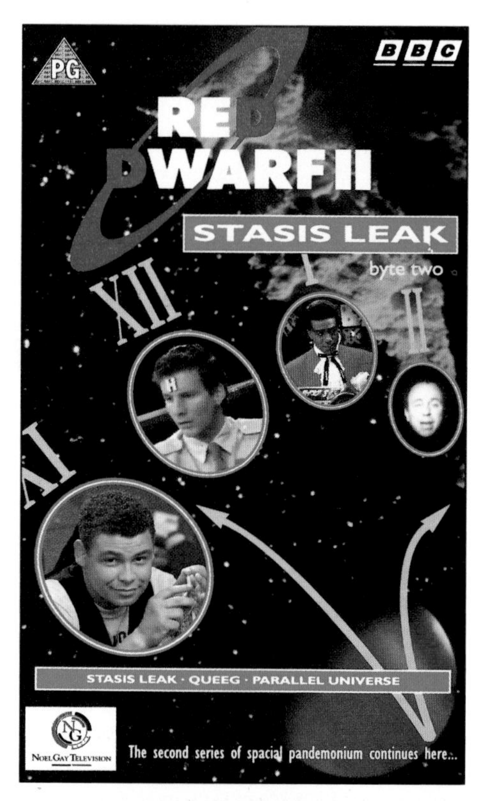

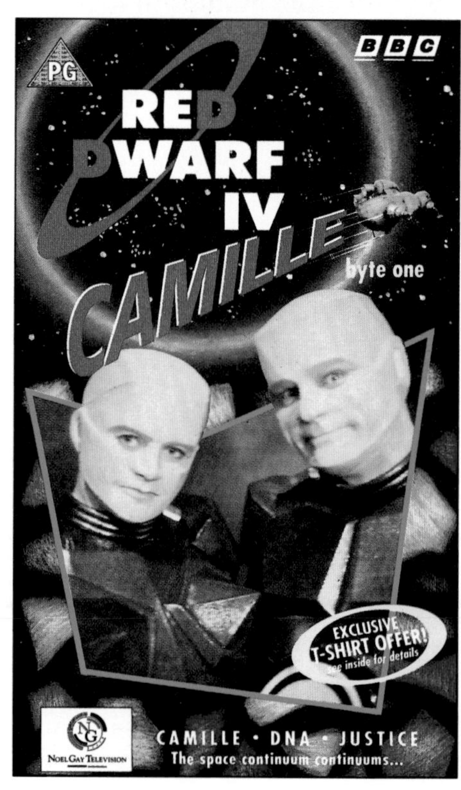

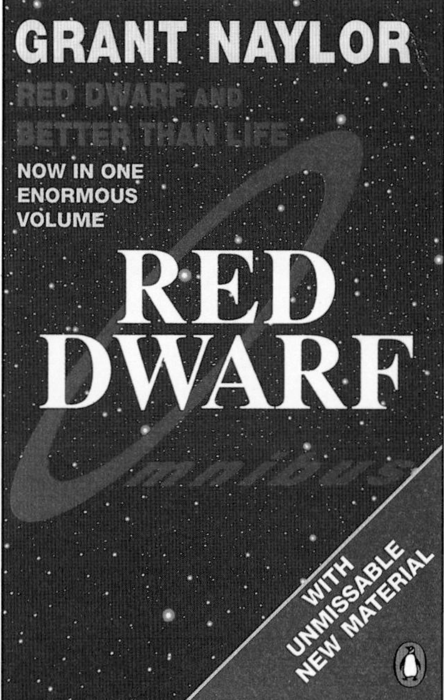


The director stayed pretty faithful to the scripts. Robert Llewellyn recalls that the main change was the sheer scale of the thing "On the English set I have to watch my head when I go through the doors. Over there everything was three foot higher. It was all much bigger." Reviews of the pilot were positive, but there is no news of a series being commissioned yet.

For British fans, however, there is better news. The sixth series is all but confirmed and should reach the screens in spring 1993. In the meantime, of course, addicts can console themselves with the multitude of merchandising that has spun-off from the series. There's an extensive range of T-shirts, badges, baseball caps and, by now, series II, III and IV ought to be available on video, with the other two to follow in 1993.

*Red Dwarf* has also gone into print, in more ways than you might imagine. First there was the Official Fan Club Magazine (details from PO Box 29, Hitchin, Herts, SG4 9TG). Now there is also the regular monthly comic, launched in spring 1992 by Fleetway Productions. The comic contains both features on the people involved with *Red Dwarf* and strips based on classic episodes. As the comic continues, it is also printing original stories inspired by the Jupiter Mining Ship crew.

Most interesting of all, however, are Grant and Naylor's novels. *Red Dwarf - Infinity Welcomes Careful Drivers* and *Better Than Life* have both been bestsellers. The books enable the team to head off in directions which TV technology and budgets don't permit. A new book is in the pipeline, but as it takes Grant and Naylor ten months to put the TV series together, it could be some time before it sees the light of day. In the meantime, there's plenty of *Red Dwarf*-abilia to keep withdrawal symptoms at bay. ■

# PRODUCTION CREDITS

| | |
|---|---|
| **Dave Lister** | **Craig Charles** |
| **Arnold Rimmer** | **Chris Barrie** |
| **Cat** | **Danny John-Jules** |
| **Holly *(seasons 1 & 2)*** | **Norman Lovett** |
| **Holly *(seasons 3 - 5)*** | **Hattie Hayridge** |
| **Kryten *(seasons 3 - 5)*** | **Robert Llewellyn** |

## SEASON 1

**The End**

| | |
|---|---|
| Captain Hollister | Mac McDonald |
| Todhunter | Robert Bathurst |
| Christine Kochanski | C P Grogan |
| Peterson | Mark Williams |
| Chen | Paul Bradley |
| Selby | David Gillespie |
| McIntyre | Robert McCulley |

**Future Echoes**

| | |
|---|---|
| Toaster | John Lenahan |
| Dispensing Machine | Tony Hawks |

**Balance of Power**

| | |
|---|---|
| Trout à la Crème/Chef | Rupert Bates |
| Chen | Paul Bradley |
| Selby | David Gillespie |
| Peterson | Mark Williams |
| Christine Kochanski | C P Grogan |

**Waiting for God**

| | |
|---|---|
| Cat Priest | Noel Coleman |
| Toaster | John Lenahan |

**Confidence and Paranoia**

| | |
|---|---|
| Paranoia | Lee Cornes |
| Confidence | Craig Ferguson |

**Me$^2$**

| | |
|---|---|
| Captain | Mac McDonald |

## SEASON 2

**Kryten**

| | |
|---|---|
| Kryten | David Ross |
| Esperanto Woman | Johanna Hargreaves |
| Android Actor | Tony Slattery |

**Better Than Life**

| | |
|---|---|
| Rimmer's Dad | John Abineri |
| Marilyn Monroe | Debbie Ash |
| Rathbone | Jeremy Austin |
| The Captain | Nigel Carrivick |
| The Guide | Tony Hawks |
| McGruder | Judy Hawkins |
| The Taxman | Ron Pember |
| Gordon | Gordon Salkilld |
| Newsreader | Tina Jenkins |

**Thanks for the Memory**

| | |
|---|---|
| Lise Yates | Sabra Williams |

**Stasis Leak**

| | |
|---|---|
| Lift Hostess | Morwenna Banks |
| Kochanski's roommate | Sophie Docherty |
| Kochanski | C P Grogan |
| Medical Orderly | Richard Hainsworth |
| Suitcase | Tony Hawks |
| Captain Hollister | Mac McDonald |
| Peterson | Mark Williams |

**Queeg**

| | |
|---|---|
| Queeg | Charles Augins |

**Parallel Universe**

| | |
|---|---|
| Ms Rimmer | Suzanne Bertish |
| Ms Lister | Angela Bruce |
| The Dog | Matthew Devitt |
| Hilly | Hattie Hayridge |

## SEASON 3

**Backwards**

| | |
|---|---|
| Waitress | Maria Friedman |
| Compère | Tony Hawks |
| Customer in Café | Anna Palmer |
| Pub Manager | Arthur Smith |

**Polymorph**

| | |
|---|---|
| Genny | Frances Barber |
| Young Rimmer | Simon Gaffney |
| Mrs Rimmer | Kalli Greenwood |

**Timeslides**

| | |
|---|---|
| Adolf Hitler | Himself |
| American Presenter | Ruby Wax |
| Gilbert | Robert Addie |
| Bodyguards | Rupert Bates |
| | Richard Hainsworth |
| Young Lister | Emile Charles |
| Young Rimmer | Simon Gaffney |
| Thicky Holden | Stephen McKintosh |
| Ski Woman | Louisa Ruthven |

| | |
|---|---|
| Lady Sabrina Mulholland-Jjones | Koo Stark |
| Ski Man | Mark Steel |

**The Last Day**

| | |
|---|---|
| Jim Reaper | Robert Llewellyn |
| Girl Android | Julie Higginson |
| Hudzen | Gordon Kennedy |

## SEASON 4

**Camille**

| | |
|---|---|
| Mechanoid Camille | Judy Pascoe |
| Hologram Camille | Francesca Folan |
| Kochanski Camille | Suzanne Rhatigan |
| Hector Blob | Rupert Bates |

**D.N.A.**

| | |
|---|---|
| D.N.A. Computer Voice | Richard Ridings |

**Justice**

| | |
|---|---|
| Simulant | Nicholas Ball |
| Justice Computer Voice | James Smillie |

**White Hole**

| | |
|---|---|
| Talkie Toaster | David Ross |

**Dimension Jump**

| | |
|---|---|
| Bongo | Robert Llewellyn |
| Mrs Rimmer | Kalli Greenwood |
| Young Rimmer | Simon Gaffney |
| Cockpit Computer | Hetty Baynes |

**Meltdown**

| | |
|---|---|
| Elvis | Clayton Mark |
| Hitler | Kenneth Hadley |
| Einstein | Martin Friend |
| Pythagorus | Stephen Tiller |
| Abraham Lincoln | Jack Klaff |
| Caligula | Tony Hawks |
| Pope Gregory | Michael Burrell |
| Stan Laurel | Forbes Masson |
| Noel Coward | Roger Blake |
| Marilyn Monroe | Pauline Bailey |

Theme song sung by Clayton Mark as Elvis.

## SEASON 5

**Holoship**

| | |
|---|---|
| Nirvanah Crane | Jane Horrocks |
| Captain Platini | Matthew Marsh |
| Commander Binks | Don Warrington |
| Harrison | Lucy Briers |
| No 2 | Simon Day |

**Inquisitor**

| | |
|---|---|
| Inquisitor | John Docherty |
| Second Lister | Jake Abraham |
| Thomas Allman | James Cormack |

**Terrorform**

| | |
|---|---|
| Handmaiden | Sara Stockbridge |
| Handmaiden | Francine Walker-Le |

**Quarantine**

| | |
|---|---|
| Dr Hildegarde Lanstrom | Maggie Steed |

**Back to Reality**

| | |
|---|---|
| Andy | Timothy Spall |
| Cop | Lenny Von Dohlen |
| Nurse | Marie McCarthy |
| New Kochanski | Anastasia Hille |
| New Lister | John Sharian |

| | |
|---|---|
| **Writers** | **Rob Grant and Doug Naylor** |
| **Producer/Director** *(seasons 1 - 4)* | **Ed Bye** |
| **Directors** *(season 5)* | **Juliet May, Rob Grant and Doug Naylor** |
| **Producers** *(seasons 3 - 4)* | **Rob Grant and Doug Naylor** |
| **Producer** *(season 5)* | **Hilary Bevan Jones** |
| **Executive Producer** *(seasons 1 - 3)* | **Paul Jackson** |
| **Executive Producers** *(season 5)* | **Rob Grant and Doug Naylor** |

| | |
|---|---|
| Visual Effects Designer | Peter Wragg |
| Costume Designer *(seasons 1 & 2)* | Jacki Pinks |
| Costume Designer *(seasons 3 - 5)* | Howard Burden |
| Make-up Designer *(season 1)* | Suzanne Jansen |
| Make-up Designer *(seasons 2 & 3)* | Bethan Jones |
| Make-up Designer *(seasons 4 & 5)* | Andria Pennell |
| Designer *(seasons 1 & 2)* | Paul Montague |
| Designer *(seasons 3 - 5)* | Mel Bibby |
| Lighting Director | John Pomphrey |
| Sound Supervisor *(seasons 1 - 3)* | Tony Worthington |
| Sound Supervisor *(seasons 4 & 5)* | Keith Mayes |
| Theme/Music | Howard Goodall |
| Vocalist | Jenna Russell |
| Videotape Editor *(seasons 1 - 3)* | Ed Wooden |
| Videotape Editor *(seasons 4 & 5)* | Graham Hutchings |
| Associate Producer *(season 2)* | Ann Zahl |
| Associate Producer *(season 3)* | Gilly Archer |
| Associate Producer *(season 4)* | Candida Julian-Jones |
| Associate Producer *(season 5)* | Julian Scott |
| Controller BBC2 | Alan Yentob |

Original Commissioning Editor BBC North